I0056355

Dropshipping:

Make $100,000 and More with Passive Income

The #1 Step by Step Guide to Make Money Online with Ecommerce, Shopify, Affiliate Marketing, Amazon FBA, Instagram, and Facebook Advertising

© Copyright 2018 - All rights reserved.

The content contained within this book may not be reproduced, duplicated or transmitted without direct written permission from the author or the publisher.

Under no circumstances will any blame or legal responsibility be held against the publisher, or author, for any damages, reparation, or monetary loss due to the information contained within this book. Either directly or indirectly.

Legal Notice:

This book is copyright protected. This book is only for personal use. You cannot amend, distribute, sell, use, quote or paraphrase any part, or the content within this book, without the consent of the author or publisher.

Disclaimer Notice:

Please note the information contained within this document is for educational and entertainment purposes only. All effort has been executed to present accurate, up to date, and reliable, complete information. No warranties of any kind are declared or implied. Readers acknowledge that the author is not engaging in the rendering of legal, financial, medical or professional advice. The content within this book has been derived from various sources. Please consult a licensed professional before attempting any techniques outlined in this book.

By reading this document, the reader agrees that under no circumstances is the author responsible for any losses, direct or indirect, which are incurred as a result of the use of information contained within this document, including, but not limited to, — errors, omissions, or inaccuracies.

Table of Contents

Introduction

I want to thank you for choosing this book, "Dropshipping: make $100,000 and more with Passive Income – The #1 Step by Step Guide to Make Money Online with Ecommerce, Shopify, Affiliate Marketing, Amazon FBA, Instagram, and Facebook Advertising."

Building a business is certainly not easy. In fact, it can seem quite daunting and scary; however, I want to congratulate you for taking the first step – that is making your mind up about starting your own business. There are several perks of being an entrepreneur and you can reap all of them, if you know what you need to do. Don't be under any misconception about the effort and time it takes to launch a business and make it successful. You need to be willing to dedicate the necessary time and effort. After all, Rome wasn't built in a day. So, if you think that you can launch a successful business overnight, you need to think again.

If you want to start a dropshipping business and earn passive income, then this is the perfect book for you. In this book, you will learn everything that you need to know about successfully launching your dropshipping business. You will learn about the benefits of passive income, the meaning of dropshipping, steps to launch a dropshipping business, and the ways to make your business successful. Dropshipping is one of the best means of earning passive income and once you are armed with all the knowledge provided in this book, you can attain all your financial goals.

Passive income can help you to earn some extra money or even substitute your regular income. The capital you decide to invest can be as high or as low as you want it to be. There are no hard and fast rules about passive earnings! You are your boss, and it can be fun! So, if you are ready to learn more about all this, then let us start without further ado.

Chapter One: Benefits of Passive Income

Why does everyone chase the idea of passive income? There are plenty of benefits that passive income offers that regular business options don't. If you want to increase your wealth, then your source of income must not just be your 9-5 job. Instead, you must focus on setting up a system of passive income. In this section, you will learn about the different benefits that passive income offers.

You Are Your Boss

If you work a 9-5 job, then you will have a boss. You will be responsible to your boss for every activity that you undertake at your workplace. Therefore, there will be a limit on the freedom that you have while you execute a task. You cannot do things on your terms, and you will always be answerable to someone. There is a strict hierarchy that you have to follow. All this restrains your creativity and doesn't let you excel. When it comes to a passive income business, you are your boss. There aren't any restrictions on what you do when you work, or how you work. When you work for others, you have to follow their rules. When you work for yourself, you can create your own rules. You can be as creative as you want, and you can establish your standards.

Less Scope for Mediocrity

In a company, more often than not, most people tend to do mediocre work. Mediocrity creeps in when you have to do something that you don't want to do. For instance, if you have to complete a task within two hours, some might take up to five hours or more to do the same work. If the average working hours are 8 hours per day and they work on a task for two hours, then they don't have anything to do for the other 6 hours. On the other hand, they will get more work if they complete one task. Therefore, they might postpone one job to limit their workload. All these reasons make the company's environment mediocre instead of productive. The passive income business is your venture, and your interests are the only ones that are involved. Therefore, you will give it your best shot. Regardless of tiredness, you feel at the end of the day, the job satisfaction you receive makes up for the rest. Since it is your brainchild, you will give it your best.

Work Environment

As mentioned in the previous point, the work environment in a company nurtures mediocrity. If everyone around you does mediocre work, then so will you. The circle you maintain has a startling effect on your life. If you want to be successful, you must surround yourself with successful people. When you opt for a passive income business, you can either choose your pack members or work as a lone wolf. You don't have to work with someone forcefully. When you can select your team or your partners by yourself, you can avoid mediocrity. You can instead opt for those who bring out the best in you.

Taxes

The income you earn from a regular job is taxable. The rate of taxation differs from one country to another. However, all posts are taxed at a certain percentage. One thing you can be sure of is that the taxes payable on the income you earn from a passive income business aren't as high as the ones applicable to your regular job. Hire the services of a professional accountant, and you can further reduce the taxes payable.

Vacation Time

If you work for someone, you will need their approval before you can go on leave. You need to submit a leave application and then wait for its sanction before you can take a holiday. If you do choose a leave, there is a loss of pay involved as well. You certainly cannot go on a month-long vacation while you work. However, when it comes to a passive income business, you can take leave whenever you want to. Your work can travel with you. So, all those beach holidays you promised yourself can finally come true! All that you need to monitor your business are a laptop and a good Internet connection. If you have these two things, you can do business from anywhere in the world. You can work at your convenience. A conventional job wouldn't let you work from anywhere. But now that your store is online, you can work from anywhere. You don't even have to worry about office space.

No Office Politics

You are responsible for all the decisions you make about the business. You don't have to impress your boss or worry about your colleagues anymore. Your opinion is the only one that

11

matters, along with the view of your target audience. You don't have to convince anyone of the idea you have. If you think your idea is profitable, then go ahead and implement it. It provides you complete autonomy of operations.

No Pink Slips

Since you are your boss, you no longer have to worry about pink slips. No one can fire you. You don't have to live under the constant fear of being fired. You wouldn't find yourself devoid of any work. Once you establish your source of passive income, you can start to earn the returns it offers with minimal work. Passive income generates money continually. There isn't a retirement age in this field, and you can work for as long as you want to.

Your Preferences Matter

With a passive income business, you can do what you enjoy. You don't have to sit in a cubicle all day long doing things that you don't enjoy. Instead, you can make the most of your creativity and put it to better use. You can transform your hobby or passion into a passive income business. It depends on your ability to apply yourself. You don't have to sit around for hours and work on a boring presentation, just because your boss asked you to!

Chapter Two: Work Ethics

Perhaps the most straightforward way you can gain financial independence is to reprogram your life in such a way that a significant portion of your income doesn't arise from active labor. Instead, it comes from passive income. The basic idea of passive income is that it refers to the money you receive with little effort, once you successfully create your source of income. There are different sources from which you can earn passive income. Some of the most popular sources are rent from real estate, royalties from patents, royalties from books, dividends from stocks, interest on other securities, affiliate marketing, and so on.

Is passive income a myth or a miracle? In fact, it is a combination of both. We can all safely agree that money indeed doesn't grow on trees and the concept of free lunch doesn't exist. What does the phrase "passive income" make you feel? There are different views about passive income and with all the views comes a lot of confusion. Quick and easy riches are what one thinks about when they hear the phrase "passive income." However, for it to be true, you must put in the necessary effort and gather all the knowledge required. Since the concept of passive income is widely misunderstood, let us first understand what passive income means.

Passive income is a form of business that has developed a process that caters to the daily requirements of business so that the owner doesn't have to. It means that certain aspects of the business can run smoothly without the need to monitor it continuously. It is a recurring stream of revenue that doesn't need the constant hands-on involvement of its creator. As a business owner, you can generate passive income only after you invest enough time and effort to create a valuable product along with automated systems to keep the business going. Passive income helps you to leverage your time in such a manner that you can create a more significant impact and help your business grow as well. During the initial stages, you must invest a lot of time on your business and create products that provide some value to customers. Passive income offers plenty of benefits that go beyond financial freedom. The streams of income you set up can help you make the most of your time, passion, creativity, as well as energy. Once you create an automated system that will scale your business, you will have plenty of time to do something else that you enjoy. It means that you can step away from your mundane work life and work on things that provide you with job satisfaction as well as a source of income. A substantial benefit that passive income offers is that it allows you the time to start other passive income businesses as well. Once your first business is up and running, you can start another one.

One thing that you must be aware of is that passive income isn't entirely passive. Certain aspects of it are passive. However, it isn't possible to run a successful business that passive. Regardless of its efficiency or the experience you possess, there will always be certain overheads that you have to take care of, update different aspects of the business, work on expanding the audience pool, and so on. The concept of a business that is entirely hands-free just doesn't exist. Maintenance of some form or the other lives in every business. Passive income isn't about finding a way to generate income without any work, and the misconception that it is a hands-off job are the two main reasons for the failure of most passive income ventures. You cannot create something, ignore it, and then expect it to flourish. Nothing on this earth works like that. If you don't water the plant, the plant will die, even if it is a cactus. The same logic applies to your business as well.

Why do a lot of passive income businesses fail?

The inherent flaw of all failed passive income businesses is the attitude of the creator. If the primary focus of the business is to quickly walk away and stop working on the business, then the business will never get the opportunity it needs to be successful. It takes dedication, passion, and hard work to run a business. If your main aim is to make a quick buck, then your business will miss out on a lot of opportunities that are essential for its success. Here are the aspects of a business that you need to focus on.

Customers

If you want to work towards a passive income business, then the one aspect of the business you must not forget is your customers. Customers need to know that you care about them and you need to earn their trust. They need to know that your business will cater to their needs. A loyal customer base can establish your authority as well as credibility. As soon as customers feel that you are not in it for the long haul, they will turn to a business that is. If earning money is your only objective, then it will show. If you don't believe in what you are offering, then your customer will not believe in it either. If you don't have any customers, then who will you sell your products to? So, you need to work hard to establish a loyal customer base for your business.

Competition

You need to remember that you are not the only player in the market. If you want to be a successful business owner, then you need to keep up with your competitors. You need to update yourself with new trends. Not just that, you also need to do some research about the factors that motivate the customer to opt for other brands. You need to make it a point to keep up with your competitors as well as the industry. If you think you can run your business without doing all this, then you are sadly mistaken.

The Right Mindset

You need to have the right business mindset if you want to build a successful passive income business. In fact, before you start any business you need to ensure that your motivations point you towards creating value for your customers. Is money your only motivation? Are you considering passive income only for personal gain? Are you going to make someone else pull all your weight and then take credit for it? If your answer is yes, then you can't become a successful passive income earner. If you want to earn money and see growth, then you need to focus on creating value for your customers. You will be in the trenches for a while and you will need to put in all the necessary hard work. You must remember that nothing worth having ever comes easy. You need to be passionate about your work and you must be willing to work hard to achieve your professional goals. If you want to be successful, then you need to create a value-centric, customer loving, and focused mindset at work.

Good Work Ethics

Success cannot be attained overnight; it needs a lot of hard work and effort. A successful business owner knows this and is willing to put in the necessary efforts. It takes time, effort, work, and discipline to create a business that will help you earn passive income. You need to have the drive and the motivation to make all this come true.

No Accountability

Having business accountability is important. When you decide to start a business by yourself, you are not accountable to anyone except yourself. No one is there to notice whether you show up for work or not, if you work hard, or even crack a new business deal. It is important that you can hold yourself accountable for the way you carry on with your business. Self-accountability isn't easy to enforce, and it is something that you need to do intentionally. Self-guilt stems from self-accountability, and you must be strong enough to deal with it. You can always approach others to make you more accountable. You can approach your friend and make sure that you aren't spiraling out of control or heading towards a meltdown. When you are the owner of a business, all the important decisions rest in your hands and you need to justify your role as an owner. You need to make sure that you take the necessary steps to make your business a success.

Financial Responsibility

There are no business partners to share your financial responsibility with and, as an entrepreneur, you must make your peace with it. The simple trick is not to let yourself get overwhelmed when you think about the various aspects of the business. Don't get stressed. If your business idea is good enough, and you can put in all the necessary efforts, then you have nothing to fear.

There are No Shortcuts

Dropshipping is a unique business model and what might work for one business owner might not work for you. Also, there is no tested secret formula to make it big with dropshipping. It is all about applying the principles of business and maximizing your profits.

There are plenty of people who promise instant wealth and success if you can just follow a "simple system" of theirs. However, the truth is that unless you are planning to rob a bank, you cannot get rich in a jiffy. Most successful entrepreneurs might have started their businesses to get rich, but no one can become successful overnight. Well, think about Facebook. During the years 2004 and 2006, it was an obscure website that was accessible only to university students so that they could network with one another. Well, now we all know where Facebook stands, don't we? It takes hard work to build a company, and it isn't easy. If you want to become successful and earn wealth from your business venture, then you need to be patient and resilient.

Focus on the Needs of Your Audience

You probably feel that you know your target audience. In today's world, there isn't one giant audience base, and instead, they are excessively segmented. So, you need to take some time to conduct the necessary research to understand the needs of your target audience. Your business won't take off if you don't cater to the needs of your target audience. Regardless of your likes and dislikes, your sole focus must be to satisfy the needs of your customers.

Ditch It

It is good to believe in your idea firmly. However, when it comes to business, it is equally important to differentiate between what is working and what isn't. If you feel that your plan isn't working, then it is foolhardy to stick to it. Instead, try to change the direction. Try a couple of different ideas and see which of those plans works.

Ask for Help

As a solopreneur, you are on your own. However, don't take this term too literally. No one is proficient at everything. If you aren't good at an aspect of the business, you can hire external help, and there is no shame in it. It is better to ask for help than to make a costly mistake.

Don't Worry

As an entrepreneur, your main aim to start a business will be to earn a profit. Being profitable is important. However, you are setting yourself up for failure if you expect to rake in profits from the get-go. It takes a while for a business to break even and, in the meantime, you must be patient. Your business needs a constant influx of funds for its growth. So, don't forget to invest back in your business.

Scalability

If you want to start a realistic passive income business, then there is one other thing that you need to concentrate on apart from your personality, work ethics, and the actual products, and that's scalability. If you want business growth and want to step away from being hands-on fully, then you need to have a solid team in place and automate the right systems. All the owners of successful passive income businesses know how to manage their time by delegating daily tasks to their team members and they have automated the processes that can help them manage their audience. The difference between a six-figure and a seven-figure business owner is the number of checks they are willing to write.

Chapter Three: Dropshipping

You may have heard of the term drop shipping, but what does it mean? How do companies use drop shipping in the word of e-commerce? Before we learn more about drop shipping, let us look at how the traditional e-commerce model works.

The Traditional E-Commerce Model

Over fifteen years ago, it was difficult for people to open a retail store since it required a lot of capital. The capital was used to buy inventory or raw material, buy a warehouse to store the inventory and a store to sell the merchandise, regardless of whether it was a brick-and-mortar store or an online store. If the owner had sufficient capital left, he would use that for marketing his products. The risk with this type of model is high since the owner will suffer a huge loss if he could not sell the inventory. Most retailers still follow this model of selling.

It is easier to start an online store these days since there are many shopping carts that make it simple for people to sell their products online. Technology and cost are no longer a barrier to entry since you can start an online store at a cost of $20 a month. E-commerce newcomers should identify a way to make a mark in the market since they do not have the same resources as big-box retailers. They should stop focusing only on the brand, and focus more on product development and customer experience. This is when they should focus on the drop-shipping model.

Drop-Shipping Model

The owners do not purchase inventory or a warehouse. They route the orders from customers to the suppliers, and the supplier will send the products directly to the customer. This will eliminate inventory risk which is an achievement for most entrepreneurs. Drop shipping is also a great way for a retailer to test new products. Instead of purchasing inventory, the retailer can list the products on the website and see which product sells. This method helps to shift the competitive advantage to marketing and customer experience from back-office logistics.

Dropshipping provides goods by directly delivering products to the customer from the manufacturer. In dropshipping, the store doesn't need to keep products in stock. As soon as the store sells a product, it will procure it from a third-party and will directly ship it to the customer. It is a method of retail fulfillment.

It doesn't take a lot of capital to start a dropshipping business, but there is a lot of work that you need to do before you can make your first sale. It isn't merely about finding the perfect product for dropshipping, but you need to find a good supplier, a fulfillment company, and various other things. In this section, you will learn about setting up a dropshipping business.

Step One: Find A Niche

The first step is to select a niche. You need to understand that you will not only be competing with other drop shippers, but various other retailers too. The well-established retailers certainly have a couple of advantages over drop shippers, but they have a significant disadvantage as well. Retailers like Walmart, Office Depot, and Best Buy tend to sell numerous products and it means that they cannot be experts in all the products that they sell. As a drop shipper, you can use their weakness to your advantage. You can focus on a specific product and become an expert. So, what is a niche? A niche refers to a specific set of products. For instance, as a drop shipper, you need to choose a specific niche. Office furniture or office desks are quite vague, and a niche product will be standing desks.

There are numerous products to choose from and it can be quite overwhelming to select one. So, here are a couple of things that you can keep in mind to find a great niche for yourself.

As a drop shipper, you need to understand that the effort it takes to sell a $10 or a $1000 item is the same. The typical margin of a drop shipper is about 20%. For instance, if you sell a $10 item, then you will earn $2 per sale. If you sell a $1000 item, then you'll earn $200 per sale. Keep this in mind when you select a product. The ideal product price point needs to be between $200 and $1000.

Penny-pinchers will look for discounts, refunds, and even return items, whereas the Rockefellers will look for boutique-level service. Both categories of customer will likely eat into your margins. The niche you select needs to resonate with the goldilocks zone. You need to look for customers who are willing to spend their money without expecting extravagant attention. The ideal customer base needs to consist of the upper-middle class section of the society. The customer needs to be comfortable with the idea of online shopping. If customers are unfamiliar or are suspicious of online shopping, then you will spend all your time trying to process orders via phone.

Drop shippers don't usually sell name-brand products. It is not possible for a drop shipper to add value to a name-brand product or satisfy the needs of a customer looking for a name brand. For instance, if someone wants to buy a PlayStation, they know that they want a PlayStation. It is unlikely that the customer will search for the "best gaming consoles" on Google. Can you name the best standing desk brands? Probably not. So, for such items it is likely that you will search on Google for the "best standing desks." A search like this will lead the customer to a dropshipping site. It is better to sell generic products because brand names are already listed on different sites.

You can also opt for all those products with limited local retailers. An ideal customer for a dropshipping business is one who will look for the perfect product instead of concentrating on savings. For instance, if someone has to buy an aquarium and finds about ten different options at the local store. Said person is not happy with the options available, so the person hops online and searches for the best aquariums.

The products that you want to choose for your dropshipping business must be light and durable instead of being heavy and fragile. As a drop shipper, you need to consider the logistics involved in the products you want to list. Shipping is the supplier's responsibility, but you are responsible for the customer service involved. Shipping issues are one of the most common issues you will face in customer service. Isn't it better to handle the customer shipping issues for something sturdy like an outdoor fireplace instead of something fragile like porcelain dolls? Also, avoid all products that require a lot of technical support while setting up.

Step Two: Identify Your Competition

Now that you have selected a niche, the next step is to check your competition. A niche without any competitors is not a good niche. So, any good niche will have some competition in it. Even if it seems counterintuitive, a niche without any competition is probably a bad sign. For instance, a good restaurant will always have a good crowd and it might even be tough to get a table at times. On the other hand, a deserted restaurant probably implies that the service or the food isn't that good. Well, it might be an undiscovered gem, but chances are that diners don't usually prefer the deserted restaurant and assume that it is deserted for a reason.

If your niche doesn't have any competition, it is likely that other businesses don't seem to think it is profitable. Maybe the niche doesn't have as many customers as you seem to think, probably the suppliers aren't good enough, or maybe the logistics are too high. Regardless of the reason, you must not waste your time on a niche that isn't profitable. If there is competition, it means that people are able to earn a profit and that's exactly what you are trying to do as well.

So, how can you find your competitors? The first thing you need to do is run a Google search on your niche and then select the Shopping tab on Google. Now, click on the products displayed and follow the links. Once you do this, you need to establish if the other sellers are drop shippers or traditional sellers. Remember that your aim is not to compete with traditional retailers. So, you need to find a niche that will help you as a drop shipper.

To establish whether your competitor is a drop shipper or a traditional retailer, you need to check their locations. If they are present in multiple locations, then they are a retailer. After you do this, you need to search for their registered address on Google Maps. If it is an online store, then you will find that it is listed as a Verizon store on Google maps.

Step Three: Identify The Best Suppliers

As a drop shipper, you will fully rely on suppliers to fulfill the orders you receive. There are some suppliers that are reliable, and they generally have an inventory of their stock and they will ship the products on the desired dates. If you find a supplier like this, then the said supplier is a top tier supplier. On the other hand, the not-so-good suppliers tend to do the exact opposite and it will simply increase your maintenance costs.

Once you identify your niche and your competitors, the next step is to identify your suppliers. You don't have to start contacting suppliers yet, but you need to know the prospects you are trying to impress. By researching your niche, you are now aware of your competitors and their suppliers who are making them money. Instead of taking a risk by approaching unproven partners, it is a good idea to use this information. It is easy to identify products and brands that are doing well for your competitors. Such products will be listed front and center on their official site to increase their visibility to the customers. They can even be listed under either the most popular or the most popular brands categories/pages.

Now, it is time for you to get working. You need to make a list of all the brands, the product names, and the stock keeping unit numbers according to your niche. You need to repeat this step for all your competitors and make a list of all the brands and products that you see often. This information will come in handy when you are looking for future suppliers.

You might wonder if there is an easier way to make a list of the top-tier sellers in your niche. Well, the suppliers that you are looking for aren't that good at marketing and that's why you need to do a little leg work. So, if you search for something like "Standing desk dropship suppliers", it is unlikely that you will find a dropshipping partner. Google search might also display supplier aggregators.

Aggregators are aware that drop shippers tend to find it difficult to find the right suppliers. So, they sell access to the list of suppliers. For a fledgling drop shipper, it might seem like a viable option to pay for an aggregator to obtain the list of suppliers. Aggregators tend to attract a lot of drop shippers who are merely looking for shortcuts and the top tier suppliers don't usually want to collaborate with someone who takes shortcuts. Top tier suppliers also don't like the idea of wasting their time screening through the list of short-cutters to find a viable dropshipping partner. So, while an aggregator might connect you to a willing supplier, it is possible that those suppliers will never be your business's top partners. There are several popular aggregators like Worldwide Brands, DOBA, and Dropship Direct.

When you start to search your competitor's websites for a list of suppliers, make a note of all the things that you like and don't like about their websites and online stores. You can use all this information when you design a storefront for your dropshipping business. If you want to know the popularity of your competitor's websites, then you can entre their URL into compete.com. You need to pay some attention to the sites that are popular and you can incorporate those features into your own site.

Once you compile a list of all the suppliers of your competitors, the next step is to verify those suppliers. The two criteria they need to meet are MAP policy enforcement and no pay-to-play.

MAP Policies

Minimum Advertised Price policies or MAP polices are the set of rules that a supplier has to protect their brand value as well as their retail partners. The lowest price at which a retailer can sell the supplier's product is known as the MAP. You need to work with a supplier who not only has a MAP policy, but also make sure that the policy is enforceable. The enforceability of MAP policies is essential because, without it, there will be a price war. A price war is the race to the bottom. As a drop shipper, your profit margins will wear out and the brand value of the suppliers will decrease. A top-tier supplier understands this and will certainly enforce their MAP policies.

You can tell whether a potential supplier enforces their MAP policies or not by simply searching for their product on Google Shopping. You must be able to see various listings of the same product. You are trying to figure out the common lowest price. For instance, if the lowest price of a listed product is $340 and if the product is not listed below this price by the retailers, then it means that the supplier is enforcing the MAP. If some listings of the product are below that price, then the supplier isn't strictly enforcing their MAP policies. For a drop shipper, the MAP also shows the lowest margin available on a product. If the margin is quite lean at MAP, then it is ideal that you look for alternatives with a higher MAP.

No Pay-to-Play

Any supplier who makes drop shippers pay a monthly or annual fee to sell their products is certainly not a top-tier supplier. It is an indicator that the supplier is more interested in earning money and not building their brand. A top-tier supplier will always value a dropshipping store since it can introduce their products to interested customers and other potential customers. Usually, you will need to either call or email the supplier to know their pay-to-play policy. Most suppliers usually provide the appropriate contact information for these sorts of enquiries on their site. There is a difference between aggregator fees and the pay-to-play fees of the suppliers.

A couple of other qualities that you need to look for in an ideal seller are:

- Whether the supplier instantly updates you about their inventory levels or not

- A comprehensive listing of their online products

- Order history

- Any customizable data feeds

- A favorable return policy

- Anything else that will help streamline and automate your work to keep your customers happy

Step Four: Build Your Website

Before any supplier will agree to partner with you, you will need a storefront. Suppliers need to be able to see that you are a worthy partner who knows how to not only talk the talk but can walk the walk as well. You don't need to be a web design wiz or a tech guru to build a dropshipping website. There are various e-commerce platforms like Oberlo and Shopify that simplify your work. It is easy to start a dropshipping website. In this section, you will learn about the different things that every dropshipping website needs to have.

The first feature that your dropshipping website needs to have is a sample product listing and brand pages. Your suppliers will want to see how their products will be listed on your store. It is easier to convince a supplier to partner with you if they can readily see their products displayed in a professional and prominent manner on your website. It also shows the suppliers that you are ready to start doing business. So, you need to build your pages in a manner that will appeal to your potential suppliers. Also, it is a good idea to include user reviews of your supplier's products and brands.

There are several companies that provide third-party monitoring as a service. A couple of companies that you can use for this purpose are Merchant Safe, TRUSTe, and Trust Guard. All these companies have badges that you can display on your website. These badges indicate to customers that they can trust your business. It might seem like an insignificant add-on, but it is quite important in the world of e-commerce. It will make your customers and your suppliers feel comfortable and safe while transacting with your business.

Ensure that the shipping and the return policies are stated

clearly and aren't ambiguous. Customers don't like discouraging return policies or any hidden shipping costs. Not just customers; even suppliers don't like ambiguous return policies since it will be bad for their business. It is a good idea to dedicate a separate page for your business's shipping and return policies.

You must always include an About Us and a Contact Us page on your website. These pages are quite easy to overlook but are critical for any business. As a drop shipper, you cannot forego either of these pages. Your customers need to know who to contact if they have any queries or any issues with their orders. Keep the About Us page brief and tell your business's story in an engaging manner. The Contact Us page needs to be easy to locate and must include a phone number, email address, the hours of operation, instant chat (if possible), and a physical address.

Step Five: Generate Traffic

Now, you need to figure out how you can generate traffic to your store. You need a detailed plan to generate and direct traffic to your site, if you want to be a successful drop shipper. Suppliers will also need to see this blueprint, because there is no point in having a wonderful store without any customers. You need to work on developing marketing strategies to achieve this objective. You can generate traffic for your dropshipping site in different ways. The first method is to use Google AdWords. Other methods include Google Product Listing Ads, Facebook Ads, retargeting, email offers, and niche blogs. Once you have a supplier onboard, or if you have a potential supplier, then they will want to know about your plan to generate traffic via marketing and advertising. So, you need to have a dedicated marketing and advertising budget.

Step Six: Register Your Business

Before you contact the suppliers to set up any dropshipping deals, you must register your business. You need to form and register your business with the appropriate authorities. Apart from income tax, dropshipping also attracts certain sales tax and sales tax exemptions. Most suppliers require the drop shipper to have an EIN or Employer Identification Number and a Sales Tax Exemption permit before they approve you as a dropshipping partner for their business.

Step Seven: Secure a Dropship Agreement

A lot of sellers merely add the supplier's products to their store and it is not good practice. Sellers have to understand that, in order to seem desirable to their supplier, they need to have a sales channel that promises good returns. Suppliers always like sellers who have high-traffic channel like blogs, websites, YouTube channels, and the like.

You need to understand that suppliers will not come knocking at your door. You need to don your sales hat and start working the phone. You need to reach out to all the suppliers you have on your list. Take some time before you decide to choose a specific seller. Remember that sellers tend to get lots of enquiries and it might take you a couple of tries before they realize that you mean serious business and that they might be a potential partner in your venture. So, you must stay positive and have an effective pitch ready.

Ensure that you contact a lot of suppliers, since not many companies might want to drop ship. It is a good idea to talk to them on the phone or even visit them in person to show your willingness to create a working relationship.

You need to set a launch date for your site. The launch date signifies that you are serious about your business proposal and that you want to start selling. A launch date also makes the supplier consider that, if your site doesn't list their products by then, then you will list someone else's products. It is important to have a timeline so that you can get started with your business. It also makes the supplier take you seriously and consider your business prospect seriously.

If all goes well up to this point, the next thing you need to figure out are your terms of payment. A supplier will obviously want to know about your payment options. Usually, drop shippers tend to pay their suppliers either upfront or they pay on terms. If you opt for the former, then you will need to pay the supplier as soon as an order is placed. If you opt for the latter, then you agree to pay the supplier at a later date (usually within 30 days). You need to be upfront and quite clear about your payment terms.

Dropshipping Tips

Work on Marketing

There are different aspects of a dropshipping business that you can automate these days. When you automate your business, you will have more time to focus on marketing and branding strategies. Designing the logo, creating the content, creating graphics, and other posts can be quite fun to do, but if you want to start raking in some profits, you need to concentrate on marketing. You need to spend some time on learning about how ads work, increase your web traffic, and also work on converting the visitors of your online store.

The two best strategies that you can use to increase web traffic to your site are ads and SEO. You need to remember that the conversion rate for most e-Commerce stores is 1-2%. It means that if the number of visitors to your store is less than 100, then you will not be able to earn any profits. The higher the traffic to your store, the greater your chances of conversion. Most drop shippers focus on ads; they might produce instant gratification and help increase sales in a short duration. If you are looking for ways to drive up your sales in the long run, then you need to concentrate on SEO. SEO increases your ranking on search engines and increases your online visibility. You can ensure that your acquisition costs stay low and reach a wider audience with a minimal ad budget if you can create blog content and start optimizing your product pages.

You must also optimize your website for conversions. If you want to compel or tempt people to make a purchase, then don't forget to use scarcity and urgency to increase the chances of sales. To ensure that you are optimizing your business's online website properly, you need to increase the instances of impulsive buying, add some favorable customer reviews as well as testimonials, and do everything you can to make the website look appealing and attractive to your customers.

Amazing Offer

An extremely important tip of dropshipping is that you need to create a compelling offer. You must not end up like all those storeowners who fail to include sales or bundles. If you notice that none of your store's products are on sale, then visitors might lack the initial motivation necessary to purchase something. If you can manage to present the right product with a good deal, then your rate of conversion will certainly increase.

Another thing that seems to work really well in the world of dropshipping is bundle deals. Whenever you decide to create a bundle deal, you need to focus on selling more items of a specific product. For instance, if you are dropshipping hair extensions, then a bundle will include more hair extensions. If your target audience seems to like the product, then they will certainly want more of it. The tricky bit is to convince your customers to not just make a purchase, but once they decide to purchase something you must upsell it. For instance, if you are ordering something and you see a combo offer on something else that interests you, then it is quite likely that you will want to buy both the items displayed.

Don't Underprice

There are certain platforms that allow you to maintain a lower product cost. You can make a profit on your sales if the cost of goods is reasonably close to the wholesale price and you can sell your products at market value. The goal of a dropshipping business like any usual business is to earn profits. If you decide to sell a $5 product, then make sure that you are charging $19 and more for it, if you want to be profitable. You must never underprice your products. Always consider different aspects of the business like the cost of the goods, marketing expenses, other business expenses, and any other expenses related to potential expansion of the business.

Don't undercut your prices merely because other dropshipping businesses are undercutting their prices. You don't have to worry about undercutting your prices as long as they are fair and are within market value. You must try to increase your average order value if you want to earn a higher return from the orders you receive. If you want to earn a higher return, then you need to come up with creative strategies that will help you upsell.

Quality Suppliers

Most suppliers that you come across are usually reliable, offer good products, and are easy to work with. At times, you might find suppliers who don't offer any of these things. Whenever you are selecting a supplier, make sure that you spend some time to thoroughly vet the supplier. As a drop shipper, the rate of success of your business depends on the quality of suppliers that you find. Make sure that the suppliers you opt for have sufficient staff on hand to ensure prompt delivery of packages. You can use a platform like Oberlo to find a reliable supplier.

Automate your Business

If you use any of the dropshipping tools like Oberlo, then several aspects of your business will be automated. If you have a full-time job or you want to generate passive income, then you need to come up with different ways in which you can automate various aspects of your business. If you automate your business, you will have more time to pursue your passions. There are different ecommerce tools that will help to automate, grow, and scale your business. For instance, Buffer lets you automate your social media posts and Kit helps you automate different marketing activities like advertising, retargeting, email marketing, and more. There are different marketing automation software available on the market that will simplify your work for you.

A Presentable Website

A critical aspect of dropshipping that you cannot afford to ignore is your business website. You need to make sure that the website is customer-friendly and easy to use. The website you create needs to appeal to customers and must not scare them off. A lot of newbie business owners start to market their business even when the home page of their site lacks certain important details like a placeholder text, a well-defined product list, and other important images. Before you decide to launch your store online, you need to take a look at the websites of your competitors in your niche. What does their website look like? What are the things they included on their homepage? Is their website easy to navigate? Do they use their logos or include their logos on their images? What are the types of pages on their website and are the pages optimized to increase conversions?

Once you look at a couple of different websites, you will have a general idea of all the things that you must and must not do. There will be certain aspects of these websites that will impress you, so try to imitate those features. Your dropshipping business's website is as important as the physical façade of a brick and mortar store. You need to make sure that your website appeals to viewers instantly and encourages them to make a purchase.

Don't Forget about Your Competition

An important business tip is that you must never forget about your competition. This tip applies to dropshipping as well. You must always be updated about the different marketing strategies your competition adopts, their scalability, and such other things. In fact, a simple way in which you can keep track of the way your competitors are doing is by following their profiles on social media. If you do this, you will have the perfect opportunity to track and measure their progress. Also, it might give you some ideas of how to change your own marketing strategy.

You can also gauge the profitability of a certain product, its demand and popularity amongst users. When you start paying attention to these details, your business will certainly do well.

Trustworthy Brand

You need to take up the responsibility for the functioning of your brand and you are the only one that's responsible for the way you represent it. If you strengthen the positioning of your brand, you can strengthen your reputation as a leader as well. Look at the different things that make your business unique. Think about the various aspects of the business that you can leverage to strengthen your brand's image. You need to concentrate on building trust by building your brand's image and increasing brand awareness amongst your target audience. Your brand is a mere extension of your business's personality. A strong brand image will certainly assist in increasing your business's value and will make it more memorable for your customers.

Chapter Four: Amazon FBA

Fulfillment by Amazon is popularly known as FBA, and is a third-party logistics service started by Amazon. It helps millions of sellers registered with Amazon all across the globe fulfil their orders. FBA provides you with the option of shipping your old as well as new products to Amazon, instead of shipping them directly to your customers. Once your products reach the Amazon Fulfillment Centers, they will handle the rest. As and when orders are placed for your products, Amazon will directly pick the stock up from these fulfillment centers and ship them to customers. They will provide you with shipping facilities, customer service once the order is delivered, and manage customer returns. It will help you save a significant amount of time, effort, and money. Many sellers who have opted for FBA have ended up saving approximately 50% on shipping costs.

The working of FBA can be summed up in one sentence: "you sell it, we ship it." A private label seller must make the most of Amazon's fulfillment network and their expertise to help in the growth of their business. Your listings on Amazon.com can make use of the free shipping services offered by Amazon, provided the bill amount is above a specified value.

The FBA listings on Amazon.com are listed and then sorted according to price, and there are no shipping costs involved if the combined value of products is above the amount of $35. The FBA listings when accompanied by the FBA logo lets customers know that the shipping, packing, customer service, and all returns are handled solely by Amazon. Fulfillment of orders even from other sales channels can be completed by using the inventory stored at the Amazon fulfillment center. The online user interface will let you manage your list and at the same time will provide the necessary direction so that the inventory can be returned at any time.

The following steps explain in brief how the process of FBA works:

Sending of Products to Amazon

You can send your products, new and used, to Amazon's fulfillment center. Seller Central uploads the details of your listings. You can decide whether you want Amazon to fulfill either partly or in whole your inventory or not. You can use FBA's Label Service to print labels, or you can also make use of PDF Labels, which are provided by Amazon. Either you can select your carrier, or you can make use of Amazon's discounted shipping facility.

As soon as the products are received by Amazon, it scans the inventory. The unit dimensions for storage are recorded. Your list can be monitored by using Amazon's integrated tracking system. The products received are cataloged and stored.

The orders placed are fulfilled by Amazon regardless of whether it has been put on Amazon.com or any other fulfillment request has been sent to sales, not on Amazon.

Web-to-warehouse, sorting system and high-speed picking system, are the technologies adopted by Amazon that let it locate the desired outcomes. Customers have the option of combining products.

The products are shipped to customers through Amazon's fulfillment centers. The products are shipped to the customer depending upon the method selected by them. The required tracking information of the products dispatched is sent to the customer. Customer service can always be contacted for orders placed on Amazon.com.

Here are some simple steps that you can follow for adding Fulfillment by Amazon to your selling on Amazon Account:

Go to the Inventory option and click on Manage Inventory.

For selecting a product that you want to include in the FBA listing, just click on the box next to it in the left column

Now go to Actions and click on Changed to Fulfilled by Amazon.

And then, all you need to do is follow the directions given to create your first shipment.

Things Needed

A Smartphone: A Smartphone is a multidisciplinary tool that finds use in almost all sectors. In the modern age, this device has proved to be a necessity rather than a luxury. A computer with an active Internet connection is also useful. As your business develops, a Smartphone will be preferred as it gives you a greater sense of flexibility.

A scouting app: A scouting app is handy for a developing business, which can be easily installed on your Smartphone.

A printer: A good quality inkjet color printer with A4 paper sheets (11×17 inches long grain paper).

Packaging equipment: This is the main component of the toolkit. As a seller, you must never run out of these tools. Stack up on your cartons, boxes, labeling sheets, tapes, and other stationery that you use for packaging your products.

How to use FBA

FBA stands for Fulfillment by Amazon. In this section, you will learn about the complete process of selling on Amazon. Follow these simple steps, and you can start to sell items using FBA.

Step 1: Create a Seller Account

The first thing you need to do is create a seller account on Amazon. If you have one, that's good, if you don't then create one for yourself. The first thing you need to choose is a Professional or an Individual account. The answer to this is simple. If you plan to sell more than 40 items a month, then you must opt for the Professional account, if not you can, use an Individual account. Amazon has a 40-items cutoff. When you use an Individual account to sell, Amazon will charge you $1 per item. If you plan to sell 40 items in a month, then you might as well pay the $40 to create a Professional account. Once you select the account type, you have to login or create an Amazon account with your choice of email. After that, you will need to provide information about the method of charge, seller information, and provide identity verification. You must opt for a credit card as your charge method. It will not be charged automatically, so you needn't worry. When you fill out the seller information, you must give your name, address, and create a Display name for yourself. The "Display name" is the name that buyers will see next to your listing of items. It can be anything that you want, but remember that it is a public name. Select a suitable display name, and it must not sound shady. You can verify your identity via a phone call or a text message. And voila! You have successfully created your seller account.

Step 2: List the Items

Once you set up your seller account, the next step is to list all the items that you wish to sell. If you aren't sure about the items that you can sell, you can start with some items you find around your home. Once you figure out the items you want to sell, you need to list them on your seller account. To add a product, you must go to the Inventory option at the top of your screen and click on the "Add Product" option. Once you select this option, you can search for the product with the help of the barcode or the product name. Unless you sell something that you manufactured by yourself, you don't have to create a new product. You can sell anything that you want. Once you select the product, you must add the product information. You need to mention the selling price of the item, the condition of the item, and whether you will ship the product yourself or whether Amazon will ship it for you. For pricing, you can enter an amount that you feel comfortable with. To price your items, you can go through the price list of similar items and fix a price accordingly. When you describe the condition of the items, try to be as descriptive as you can and be honest too. Select any of the options like "acceptable," "good," "new," or anything else accordingly. However, it is better if you offer an additional description. Be honest about the condition that the item is in and don't exaggerate. You don't want the customer to return your item or ask for a refund, do you? So, be honest if you're going to avoid negative reviews. Since you want to use the FBA option, you must select the same for the shipping method. If you are using FBA for the first time, then Amazon will provide you with a registration screen with the terms and conditions that are applicable. Go through this page carefully and accept the terms if you agree.

Step 3: Convert Your Items

You need to convert your items to FBA items. You might wonder why you must do this if you selected the FBA option in the previous step. Well, the answer is quite simple. Amazon has specific policies and to use their FBA service you need to convert your items to Fulfillment by Amazon items. To convert your items, you must go to your inventory, select the "manage inventory" option. You will find a drop-down list of "actions" and select the "Change to Fulfilled by Amazon" option. Once you select this option, you will find two preferences. The two options available are 'FBA Label Service' and 'Sticker-less Commingled Inventory'. If you want to sell a new item, then you can use the second option.

In this, Amazon will mix your units with those of other sellers who sell similar items. If someone places an order for a similar item like yours, then Amazon may ship the buyer a unit from either your stock or some other seller. The FBA Label Service is quite important. It allows Amazon to place a label on your items and you don't have to do it yourself. If you don't want to print your labels, then this is the best option for you. It costs about 20 cents per item if you avail this service. If you want to increase your profit margin, then you can label the products by yourself. Once you select either of the options, you will be given two choices by Amazon. The first option is "Convert Only" and the second option is "Convert and Send Inventory." If you select the convert only, then you can add more items to your inventory before you ship it to the Amazon warehouse. After you complete all these steps, you will notice that your items will appear under the heading of "Amazon-Fulfilled Inventory."

Step 4: Shipping Plan

If you select the "Convert and Send Inventory" option, or if you have just added another option, the next step is to create a shipping plan for the items. You need to list the "Ship from" address and the packing you require. The two types of packing available are individual items and case-packed items. The choice depends on the kind of product or item you want to sell. Once you create your shipping plan, the next step is to add the items. I am assuming that this is the second item that you added so that you will see two items. Now you must select both the items or as many items as you wish to sell. You must repeat the same process for all items you want to add, and, in the end, you must select the "add to an existing shipping plan" option instead of a "create a new shipping plan" option.

Step 5: Ship Your Products

Now that you have listed all the items, you must ship them. To send your products or units, you need to go to the inventory, click on the "Manage FBA shipments" and click on the "Continue with shipping plan." Enter the number of items that you want to ship. If your items require any prep, select whether you want Amazon to do the prep or not. Lastly, you must choose if you or Amazon can label the product. When the products are ready to be shipped, weigh them once. Print the labels and stick them on the package. After this, they are prepared to be sent and drop them off at a local UPS.

Step 6: Sell Your First Item

It is the most straightforward step of all. Once you ship the package to Amazon and they receive it, your items are now officially available for purchase. Now, all that you need to do is wait for a buyer to make a purchase. If the product you decide to sell is one of the popular ones, then you will be able to sell it within a week or two.

By now you will have sold a product. If not, at least your products are now available on Amazon.

Chapter Five: Email List and Follow-Up Emails

If you want to successfully market your business, then you need to have an engaged email list. You might have something valuable to offer your potential customers, but how can you make them give you their email address? Fortunately, there are a couple of different ways in which you can grow your email subscriber list. In this section, you will learn about all these methods.

A Sign-Up Button

It isn't necessary that everyone who reads your emails is on your email list. For instance, if you share your email address on social media, it's not necessary that all your followers will be on your email list. People might also forward your email to their friends. If you know that you put some valuable content in the email, then people will share it. So, whenever you send out a new newsletter, you can get subscribers. To make it easy for visitors to sign up, you can add a join my email list link to any of the emails you send.

Sign-Up Form on Your Website

Your website will be the first contact for a lot of people who want to do business with you. You must not miss this opportunity to connect with new visitors. You can include a sign-up form on your website so that all those who are interested can sign up immediately.

At Events

If you host any events where people can register or where they need to purchase tickets for in advance, then you can even collect contact information at such events. In fact, it is the perfect time to encourage people to subscribe to your email list. When you collect information from registrants, it gives you an opportunity to communicate with the attendees.

Industry Tradeshows

Industry events, conferences, or even tradeshows are a great place to increase your email list. Such events provide you with the opportunity to connect with new customers as well as similar businesses. You can put up a sign-up list at the conference and even on your website.

Existing Database

Never overlook your existing database of contacts that you have with you. It can include your colleagues, acquaintances, friends, or even family members. It is a good place to start growing your email list. Initially, your email list might just include your friends, and family members, but after a while it will grow. Take the feedback that you receive from your existing contacts and make the necessary changes to move ahead. You can even make them spread the word about your business.

Downloadable Whitepaper

You can use a couple of lead magnets to grow your email list. A simple way in which you can grow your customer relationships is to offer them a lead magnet like a whitepaper or any other educational resource in exchange for their email address. Ensure that the content you offer is unique, resourceful, and entertaining. It must engage and encourage your audience to subscribe to your list. Or perhaps you can offer a glimpse at a whitepaper or any other educational resource and provide the rest to the reader once they sign up. It is a simple way to gather new leads.

Sign-Up With Their Phone

You need to make it convenient for your existing and potential customers to join your email list by enabling them to sign-up using their phone. For instance, the Text-to-Join tool of Constant Contact enables people to join your email list by sending a text message along with a code that is unique to your business.

Membership Forms

If you have plans of offering membership, then you can include a sign-up option on such forms. It will encourage people to sign up and it will not even look like you are trying hard to grow your email list.

Social Media

You can include a sign-up page on your business's Facebook page. Social media is a wonderful tool that you can use to increase your reach. You can encourage and prompt your followers and fans to subscribe to your mailing list by including a simple sign-up form on your Facebook page. You can even include a sign-up form on your Instagram page as well. The one thing that you need to ensure for this technique to work is that you post exceptional and engaging content on your profiles. If your profile impresses the viewer, then it is quite likely that they will be willing to sign up for your email list as well.

Facebook ads

You can run a Facebook ad to increase your business's reach. You can use Facebook ads to grow your email list. Instead of using a Facebook ad to drive traffic to your page, you can run an ad to encourage people to sign-up for your email list.

Exclusive Access

Exclusivity is the best way to grow you email list. If you can offer something that will interest your audience, that they will not find anywhere else, then it will encourage them to sign-up for your email list. So, you need to be able to create useful and interesting content that is unique to your email list.

Now that you are aware of the different techniques that you can follow to grow your email list, the next step is to implement these tips.

Chapter Six: Sales Funnels

A sales funnel is the path that enables a potential customer to move from the stage of awareness of the product, to interest, desire, and finally to make a purchase. It is important that you create a sales funnel for your business. It might seem like a small aspect of a business, but it has the potential to increase your sales. A sales funnel is like a business plan that leads a prospect from their "I don't know" phase to the "let us do business" stage. A sale doesn't happen, and at times, the potential customer needs a little encouragement to go ahead and make the purchase. In this section, you will learn about the different steps that you can follow to create a sales funnel for your business.

Identify Your Prospects

Before you can devise a plan to encourage a potential prospect to do business with you, the first thing you need to do is identify your prospects. Your goal is to direct the interested parties from the wide end to the narrow end of the funnel. So, the first thing that you need to do is determine who your ideal customer will be. You can create a questionnaire to help you move along. For instance, if you want to dropship standing desks, then who will be your target audience? Is it just for businesses or even private individuals? What is the demographic of your target audience? Who will the product appeal to? Ask yourself a couple of simple questions and you will have an idea of your target audience.

Qualify Your Prospects

A person might fit into your profile of an ideal customer, but it doesn't mean that such a person is necessarily an ideal customer. Maybe someone has a business, but they don't like standing desks, then such a business might fit all your requirements of an ideal customer but their lack of desire for the product you offer disqualifies them. So, you need to spend some time and qualify your prospects after identifying them. It is quite simple to qualify prospects. You can conduct a survey or a poll; you can even talk to people about their needs or you can create a product that you know will appeal to your target audience. Without the right audience, you cannot increase your sales even if you have a wonderful product.

Apply the Fundamentals

Your sales funnel is a means to direct your prospects as well as potential customers to your business to finalize a sale. For instance, if you have a blog that you post on daily, you can promote the blog on social media to increase the customer's attention to your business. Once your prospects land on your blog, you can encourage them with an offer to obtain their email address. You can then start to send out emails regularly to encourage those prospects to make a purchase. One thing that you can do is start by selling something that is easily affordable to your prospects like a $20 item. Once they make a purchase, you will have a list of confirmed buyers. Once you have this list, you can start to send them a list of higher-priced products to drive the prospects deeper into the sales funnel.

Establish the Sales Funnel

The best way in which you can plan your sales funnel is to start backwards. So, if you have a $200 product, then you will need to find those people who are willing to spend that kind of money for the benefits the product offers. People will spend money on a product you offer, only if they trust you. So, you need to slowly build some trust. A backward plan for a sales process will start with an expensive product, a mid-range product, an introductory product, free informational piece or a sample, an email sign-up campaign, blog conversation, and social media interaction.

The key is to understand the needs of your customer and to meet those needs.

Chapter Seven: Blogging

Words are said to be more powerful than swords and bullets. Words, when employed cleverly, can win you not just money but also wars and countries. Such is the power of words alone that they are said to be one of the most influential factors in any transaction. Why must your business be deprived of the blessing of words?

Start a blog about your business. A business blog is usually a place where you not only advertise your products and services but also attract customers via the same. A blog can provide all or any of the following kinds of information:

The description of the exact products and services your online business has got to offer. This blog can use the power of creativity to make sure that not only are your customers informed but attracted as well.

Know the pros and cons of a particular product or service. Your blog is supposed to be a platform where the general public gets to know about the unbiased opinions about your business. Do not always praise and boast about your successes. Admit defeats by warning your customers against some slip-ups you might have made.

Guidance

The best form of help you can provide via a blog is guiding your clients regarding any queries they might have about a product or a service. Open a hotline number that is to be managed by an employee the entire day. Any aggrieved or curious person can contact this number in case they've got a complaint or are simply curious.

Reviews

Invite people to give reviews about your business. If you have worked decently so far and your business has been in the market for a fair amount of time, people are bound to have liked your service. Why refrain from exploiting their satisfaction to further gain in the popularity sector? Allow people to leave star ratings and good feedback by including a box for feedback on your website.

Your blog need not necessarily be about your business alone. It can be about the general market as well. You can review other businesses and the entire market if you have the time, thereby establishing a good platform for customers to come and get honest views not just from consumers but also from an established business person, which is you.

Blogging is a great way to make sure that your business reaches out to people and, because everything is online, you do not have to sweat it out in the sun hanging posters and running for billboard authorities. Hire a good web designer who can set up a well maintained website for you to operate.

Make sure you are well acquainted with the functions of all the features of the blog and your website. Do not write just for the sake of it; write so as to keep the average customer informed and entertained. Your graph keeps going up as long as you are regular with your blog. When you are irregular, people lose interest after a while, and that affects your credibility as a businessman since they cannot trust you to deliver on time and at a uniform frequency. Moreover, they also lose out on getting updated with the recent developments in the product or service they have subscribed to or bought from you. These days anyone who has an internet connection has got a blog of his own and does not require any official publication to let people know his or her views on things, ranging from life issues to scientific ones. Starting a blog is a great booster to your online venture.

Search Engine Optimization

Have you ever tried to look up a specific thing on Google? If yes, then you must be aware of how Google shows you results, yes? Say if you typed in the search bar "Tiger", it will show you all possible results related, remotely or otherwise, to the animal tiger. However, if there has recently been a warship named 'Tiger,' and the same has caused ripples in the social media world, then this piece of news is going to appear before any other. Have you ever thought as to why the results are arranged the way are? The answer is Search Engine Optimization.

The idea is very simple. When you write about your products or services, you have to be as simple as a worker bee. You cannot afford to clutter your blogs with content that has very little to do with what the core of your business is or is supposed to be. Be precise when talking about your product. If you have an associated website to your online business, make sure its content does not beat around the bush and does not contain matter that is irrelevant to the fundamental principles of your business. Search Engine Optimization is a great way to regulate, which search appears first and which one appears last when an innocent consumer decides to find out about your merits on the Internet.

Blogging is quite a trendy activity these days. A blog will help increase the reach of your business in the marketplace. Your business is a powerful system that can satisfy the needs of a target audience. Before your products can satisfy anyone's wants or needs, you need to supply your business with a constant flow of interested customers. So, how do you do this? You can do this by running a blog. A blog will help direct traffic to your business's site as well.

What are the benefits of blogging? Blogging will help direct more traffic to your business's site through SEO. You can include call-to-actions or CTAs in your blog posts to generate new leads for your business. If you share quality and engaging content, then it will improve your authority in the concerned field. It is also a great means to connect with your audience. Apart from all this, it also acts as a feedback machinery to receive feedback from all those who visit your blog. Here are the steps that you can follow to start blogging.

Create Content

The first step is to create good content for your blog. If you use a free service to host your blog, then you can go through the tutorial it offers to go through the initial stages of setting up a blog. If you host your site, then you need a little experience with web design to customize your blog. Content is king, and you need to have compelling content if you want to earn money from your blog. You must come up with new and innovative topics to write about. If not a new topic, then you must offer some fresh perspective on existing subjects. Learn to present information compellingly. The writing style of your blog must be easy to understand and enjoyable for the reader. If you have a flair for writing, then this is the perfect outlet for your creativity. You need to post regularly, and you must update your blog frequently. If you promise to post one post every alternate day, then make sure that you stick to your promise.

Use Social Media

Social media is a powerful tool. Where are your target audience these days? How do they spend their time and how can you find them? How can you attract your target audience to your business? Well, social media channels are the answer to all these questions. Almost everyone is active on one social media platform or the other these days. So, you need to share valuable content with your target audience on social media.

Guest Posts

If you want to increase your blog's reach, then you can contribute to other blogs present in your niche with relevant content that will interest your audience. You need to comprise a list of blogs that you can approach with your proposal. You can write free guest posts for these blogs in return for a backlink to your business site or your own blog. The growth of your blog is directly proportional to the growth of your business.

Feedback

You can use your blog to obtain feedback from your customers and interact with them. After all, all those who regularly follow your blog have mostly purchased something from your site. At the end of the blog post, you can encourage your readers to share their opinions and give their feedback. You can work on the feedback you receive. If you receive any positive feedback, it will encourage other readers to make a purchase. Negative feedback on the other hand will help you identify the areas of your business that you need to improve.

Marketing Your Blog

Now that you have a blog, the next step is to market your blog. You cannot gain new readers if you do not promote and market your blog. When it comes to promoting your blog, you can start with a couple of keywords for every post. Keywords are quite relevant, and they help with the SEO ranking of your blog posts. So, every post that you write ensures that you select a couple of keywords that people tend to use frequently to increase the visibility of your work. Not just that, it will also help to improve your audience. There are different keyword research tools that you can use, like Google Keyword Research. Once you find a couple of keywords that you can associate with your blog posts, you need to include them in critical places. The important places to add keywords are the titles of posts, headers, and even in a couple of sentences on your blog. Change the settings on the platform such that the URL of your blog posts include the title and not the date on which it was posted. The title of your blog posts must be descriptive yet brief.

Social media has become an integral part of today's world. Whenever you post something new on your blog, make sure that you post links to your blog on different social media platforms. The idea is to increase traffic to your blog as much as you possibly can. To increase blog traffic, you need a larger audience. What can be better than social media to find a broader audience? You need to be active on blogging platforms and start to follow other related blogs as well. Paid adverts are an excellent way to market your blog. However, it is better if you can gain natural leads instead of artificially generated leads. Try to use ads on Facebook, StumbleUpon, or even Google AdSense.

Chapter Eight: Market Research and Niche Products

If you want to become a successful seller, then you must think about niche marketing and selling. You must consider starting your niche store. A niche is a small part or the sub-market of a broader market. Niche stores are usually very competitive, and they have the right demand for the product they are selling.

Find a Niche

You will need to find a niche that suits you and the requirements you have in mind. When you do find a niche that you like, type the same into the search bar provided on eBay. It will help you to check out the competition that exists. Since you are just getting started with niche selling, make sure that there isn't too much competition. If not, you will have a tough time selling. Look into different sub-categories of niches as well. Even if it sounds eccentric, it might be lucrative. Do a lot of research and don't just stick to the most obvious options that are available online.

Select a Product

You will need to select a product that you want to sell! eBay and Shopify have numerous sellers listed on it. Opening up your niche shop is an excellent idea if you were always interested in starting your own business.

Your Competition

Make it difficult for your competition to offer the same products that you are offering. Or make your pricing strategy attractive. You must have a unique selling point or USP that will differentiate you from all the other sellers within your niche. Also, make sure that the market is large enough for you to survive.

Setting Up Your Store

There are some ways in which you can personalize your storefront. This personalization is of great importance to ensure that your store stands apart from the rest; you can quickly grab the attention of potential customers, and promote your brand. You can add a banner to your storefront. A banner is a graphic that will run across the page of your store, and you can create this without much difficulty by making use of graphics software and programs like Picasa, Photoshop, Windows Paint and so on. Always include a shop title and shop announcement. Your shop title will be similar to a tagline, and it will sum up in brief what your shop is all about. Shop announcement is different from a shop title; this will be appearing on the banner, providing information about the products you sell, the materials used, and your artistic philosophy, if any exists. Your shop announcement can also be made use of for broadcasting about any upcoming events. There are different types of items that you might sell. If you are selling products like notebooks, magnets, pens, picture frames, then you can organize this as stationery, and you can make use of further sections like size, type, material or price.

When you start selling your products or goods in your eBay or Shopify store, you might wonder about the amount you must charge customers for your items. If you want to have a profitable online shop on these platforms, then you will need to be comfortable going over some numbers and doing a little math regarding your pricing strategy. There are two simple formulae that you will need to learn for this, and they aren't difficult.

The first one is:

(Materials+Labor+Overhead) x2 = Wholesale price

And the second one is:

Wholesale price x2 = Retail price.

But the cost of shipping isn't included in this. The second formula can be adjusted according to your convenience. When you multiply the wholesale price by 2, it will provide the retail price. At times, sellers opt for a number higher than two like 2.5 or 3 for determining their retail price, provided that the market is willing to bear such an expense.

Product photos that are well photographed can act as a catalyst for promoting sales for your eBay store, but you needn't hire a professional photographer to do this. You can very well compose your photos; here are some pointers that will help you portray your product in the best possible manner. All you need is a little bit of artistic flair, some patience, and the following guidelines. You must angle your camera; this means tilting the camera a little so that it will put the subject matter slightly off center and create some movement and flow. It will produce a picture that is more intriguing. Make sure that you fill the frame with your product so that it not only seems more appealing, but potential buyers can also see how well crafted your product is. For highlighting your piece dramatically and adding a little bit of panache to it, you can blur the background so that the focus automatically shifts to your product. Always frame your picture with a darker element. You can group your products, especially if you are into designing or creating itsy bitsy products, then for attracting attention, you can arrange several products together so that the buyer can see how cohesive your products are together. Make use of the rule of thirds. It is a straightforward rule; you will need to divide the scene that you are photographing into nine parts by making use of two horizontal and vertical lines like a tic tac toe grid. It will help in piquing the interest of the viewer.

An item title is like a good headline for a product, and it needs to be designed in such a manner that it will grab the buyer's attention and get them to want to read more about that particular item. You will need to keep it short and contain it to within 155 characters inclusive of spaces. Describe things at the beginning of the item title so that it will help in improving the chances of searching for a specific item.

Chapter Nine: Customer Service

You need to ensure customer satisfaction if you want your business to grow. Customer service doesn't start after a sale, but it goes on even before a customer makes a purchase. It takes some extra resources, a little time, and money to deliver good customer service. All this extra effort certainly goes a long way in enhancing your customer's overall experience with your business. There is no other form of publicity that works better than the good old word-of-mouth publicity. A happy customer will not only be a repeat customer but will also recommend your business to others. In this section, you will learn about the different aspects of providing good customer service.

Respect

The first thing you need to do is always treat your customers with respect. Treat customers with respect regardless of their attitude towards your business. After all, customers are essentially the heart of any business. Irate customers can be quite troublesome to deal with, but you need to deal with them patiently and calmly. In fact, an irate customer might also become one of your most loyal customers.

Feedback

Feedback, regardless of it being a positive or negative, is quite important to your business. You need to follow up on any feedback you receive. If it is a positive one, reply to it promptly with a thank you. If it is negative feedback, make sure that you follow it up with a solution and take the necessary action.

Feedback is a great opportunity to display your customer service skills and increase the level of customer satisfaction.

After Sales

Your work doesn't end once you make a sale. You need to make sure that you inform the customer that their support was invaluable to your business. You need to thank them for doing business with you and this is the opportunity to create a touch point. You can use this opportunity to introduce your customers to other products listed on your business website.

Customer Complaints

Complaints are part and parcel of any business. You need to deal with them in an effective and positive manner. Ensure that you listen to your customer's complaints, apologize for any trouble it caused them, and offer them an appropriate solution. You must not blame the customer. Think of it as an opportunity to make improvements to your business.

Returns

You need to create a standard procedure to deal with customer returns. If a customer receives a defective product and wants to return it, there needs to be a procedure they can follow. You must be able to replace the defective product within the stipulated time according to your terms of service.

Customer's Needs and Wants

You need to understand the specific needs and wants of your customer. To do this, you need to reach out to them. If you know what your customer wants, you can offer better service.

Empathy

Empathy is the ability to understand what others feel. You need to empathize with your customers. Whenever you empathize with your customers, it will create a bond between the two and will make your customer feel welcome.

Listen

You must understand that a customer is reaching out to you because he or she wants to be heard. So, you need to listen and understand their issue, empathize with them and address the issue. It means that you must always read their messages thoroughly and understand what they are trying to say.

Rapport

You need to build a rapport with your customers if you want them to stick around. It means that you can highlight your shared interests and passions to make your business seem friendly to customers. A happy customer is an invaluable asset for any business.

Employees and Staff

If you have employees and staff working along and for you, then you need to value them. They are your first customer and you need to treat them well to make sure that they are happy. If they are happy, they will serve your customers well. The attitude of employees dictates their interactions with customers.

Customer Service Standards

You need to set certain service standards. It isn't just about drawing up the standards, but it is also important that your staff comprehends them. Draw up a written document dictating the way customer's expectations need to be handled and can help your business.

These standards will also help gauge the way your employees are dealing with customers. There are different training programs you can use to train your employees to deal with customers. An excellent staff is important for the growth of any business.

Customer Expectations

You need to clearly let your customers know all that you can and cannot do. Once you make this clear, it will help customers establish certain expectations. Ensure that your standards as well as policies are clearly mentioned in the descriptions of all the items that you sell.

FAQ or Help Page

You need to create a FAQ page or a Help page on your website. These pages will answer the immediate questions that a customer might have. There so many instances when customers get confused about shipping, billing and delivery policies. Ensure that you have a reply to all these topics on the FAQ page. You need to make sure that you include contact information on the help page. Customers need to know who to approach in case of any troubles they face.

It is important that you concentrate on providing good customer service. Follow the simple tips given in this chapter to improve your customer service and relations.

Chapter Ten: Branding

So far, you have been working on building the foundation of your business. Give yourself a pat on the back for coming a long way. Without a unique identity, a business is not complete. Branding helps carve an identity for your business. Branding lends personality to your business. For instance, think about your favorite company for a moment. You probably are familiar with their logo, their advertisements, and maybe the slogans they use. These are all important elements of branding. You need to make your business memorable and that's the only way in which you can separate your business from your competitors.

A brand is a company's identity. No two individuals are alike and, similarly, no two businesses are alike, and brand helps make this differentiation. A brand is your business's personality. A lot of businesses seem to think of branding as a mere afterthought. If your business doesn't have a brand, then it will not be memorable to your customers. A lot of fledgling drop shippers give up and quit because of this. The reason is that they don't spend enough time on branding. There are two aspects of branding and they are internal branding and external branding.

Internal Branding

Regardless of whether you are a solopreneur or if you have a small team of staff, your business needs internal branding. It might seem like a small aspect, but don't ignore it. Internal branding helps you understand what your business stands for.

It is a means of saying that the business focuses on its customers. Your customers cannot see internal branding, but the public presence of your business will reflect the internal attitude of your business. Internal branding helps facilitate optimal work environment and ethics. The mission statement along with the list of values are the two ways to implement internal branding.

Mission statements describe the primary objective of your business. The mission statement of Nordstrom is "to give customers the most compelling shopping experience possible" and that of JetBlue is "to inspire humanity – both in the air and on the ground." A mission statement isn't a business cliché, but it can help stir up some good PR. Mission statements will guide all those involved in your business in all aspects of work. It can improve your morale, establish a positive work environment, and improves communication as well. Take a look at the above-mentioned mission statements; they are all about what the company can do for customers. If you make the mission statement all about your business, then it will not work. Not a lot of drop shippers take the mission statement seriously.

You might not realize it, but a lot of companies work according to their mission statement. For instance, IKEA's primary goal to help people create a better everyday life influences everything they do, from their product design to the store layout. This is the sort of internal structure that you must strive to create for your dropshipping business. It is important that you establish internal branding before you think about working on external branding. Internal branding is like the foundation of a construction, and without a foundation you cannot erect a façade. While drafting the mission statement, there are a couple of things that you must keep in mind.

The mission statement must not be self-serving. You need to put your customer first and don't go overboard using "we" in the statement. Don't get caught up in your ambition and lose track of the customers you need to cater to. Always think about the verbs you can use in the mission statement. You need to include the verb and the recipient in the mission statement. Most mission statements start with "To __." You need to include some verb like inspire, give or offer and add your intended recipient (customers) in it as well. Think about the reasons why your business does what it does. Every business needs a fundamental reason for its existence. Think about the purpose of your business and include it in your mission statement.

You can make a rough draft of all the possible mission statements and the one statement that best summarizes your goals is your answer. You might also have to change your mission statement as your business grows. Your mission statement must always be in sync with your business objectives and aims.

External Branding

External branding includes various things like your logo, customer support emails, and your social media presence. Your logo and your business website are amongst the first things that a customer will see. So, it is paramount that you make a good impression. Next, you need to concentrate on the style and tone of the content you use. Text and media are a means of communicating with your customers and you need to ensure that all these aspects are in sync with your business objective. In this section, you will learn about the different elements of external branding.

Logo Design

There is a reason why companies shell out a lot of their money on logo design. A logo is not a mere design, but it is a way in which people can instantly recognize your business. Take a moment to think about all the logos that are committed to your memory. Human beings are visual creatures, and if you see a logo that you love, it will be committed to your memory. You can use the logo for your social media accounts, on business cards, your email profile, and even for your storefront. The first thing that the customer will see is your business logo, so you need to make it as good as it possibly can be. A good logo might be slightly expensive and that's why a lot of entrepreneurs tend to opt for a logo that they can make it themselves. Unless you are a qualified designer, it is a good idea to hire someone to design your logo.

Website

If you want to use a website of your own for dropshipping, then you need to concentrate on your website design. Your website is similar to the storefront of a brick and mortar store. Your website reflects your business. So, you need a website that will give your business prominent web presence. You know that website design is important, but how many of the websites that you visited in the past week do you remember? You probably don't remember many and that's because an average website doesn't give website design the credit it deserves. Try to avoid a generic look for your site. Your website needs to attract customers and must not kill your rate of conversion. The website needs to appeal to your target audience and it needs to further your business goals.

Whenever you are designing your website, you need to make

sure that you are integrating your branding into the site. Your website is a mere extension of your business. So, the theme, fonts, colors and the images that you use on the website need to be consistent with your brand. The website design needs to be memorable and must be unique. You can either build the site yourself or hire someone to do it for you.

Content

Once you have figured out the other aspects of external branding, you need to concentrate on your content. You need to make sure that a fancy website with boring content will not be memorable. You need content for your ads, marketing content, social media posts, product descriptions, and anything else like blog posts or videos and the like. You need to create exceptional content that is consistent with your branding. Good content always helps with conversions. So, you need to make sure that you provide unique, valuable, and interesting content for your audience.

Chapter Eleven: Print on Demand

Physical products like t-shirts make a great product. You can use the services of a fulfillment company to handle the time-consuming parts of the business such as printing, order fulfillment, and even shipping. Most print-fulfillment companies don't have a high start-up cost, and you don't need much of inventory either. You can also have your products dropshipped. Yes, dropshipping comes in handy in this business. You can sell products and have the same delivered to your customer directly from the manufacturer. Passive income from physical products takes some time and effort. In this section, you will learn about how you can create a t-shirt printing business for yourself sans inventory. That does sound amazing, doesn't it?

Step 1: Storefront

You might have brilliant designs for t-shirts, but your designs will need a home too. There are multiple commerce solutions to create a virtual storefront for yourself. A couple of things that you must consider while you select a platform for yourself are the monthly costs involved, transaction fees, accessibility, options to customize, and its ability to be integrated with other platforms like email services and social media. Shopify is amongst the best platforms available today. You can quickly create a virtual storefront for yourself. You can have a brand name, design a logo for the brand, and customize your storefront as much as you want.

Step 2: Print Fulfillment Company

There are different fulfillment companies for you to choose from. You can try Printful or something like Print Aura or Scalable Press. They offer different styles of t-shirts to choose from and can be easily integrated with other e-commerce platforms. Check their terms and conditions, fees chargeable, and other policies. After all, the print fulfillment company will do most of your work for you. So, you need to make sure that you select the right provider.

Step 3: Connect the Storefront to the Fulfillment Company

Now that you have an e-commerce platform for your storefront and a print company to fulfill your orders, the next step is to integrate these two. You must not skip this step, or else your requests will not be sent for printing and delivery. You can configure the settings for shipping costs, the shipping address, a customer service email address (other contact information), and invoices too.

Step 4: Customer Service Page

Even though you don't have to order the fulfillment of your product personally, you need to make sure that the customer has a place for grievance redressal. A couple of pages that you must create include a page for exchange and refund policies, contact, FAQs, shipping and tracking, and size charts. Carefully go through all the different procedures that the print company has about handling issues and complaints. Your policies will depend on their policies. For instance, if the print fulfillment company needs photographic evidence to deal with a problem, then make sure that your store policy does too. Try to be as comprehensive as you can when you create these pages. The more detailed the information you provide, the fewer problems you will run into.

Step 5: Design

It is the fun part of the business operation. Now is the time to unleash all your creative ideas about t-shirt designs and designing. Go through the design guidelines of the printing company before you start to design the t-shirts. They tend to offer different templates so that you can place and design the t-shirts properly. It will be a waste of time and effort if you design something that the fulfillment company cannot print. There are different guidelines that the printing company will provide regarding saving and uploading files. You must pay attention to the various specifications they provide. You can use tools like Adobe Illustrator, Canva, or even Snappa to design t-shirts.

Step 6: Create a Mockup

Now is the time to test your design. You must know how the finished product will look, don't you? Well, create a mockup of your design, and you can see for yourself. It will also help you to make any necessary changes. You need to remember that the mockup will closely resemble the finished product you offer your customers. Make sure that it is of good quality and is something that the customers will want to purchase.

Step 7: Upload Your Designs

Carefully follow the instructions that the fulfillment company provides when you upload your designs and link them to each of the individual listings. You can set printing options as well as the sizes here. If you have multiple options or designs you want to sell, then you must do the same for each item. You can upload a mockup of the design.

Step 8: Order Samples

It is another epic milestone for your business. It is a critical step, and the success of your t-shirt designing business will depend on the print fulfillment company's ability to deliver. Place an order for a sample and see how it is delivered. Pay attention to the quality of the t-shirt, the quality of the print, the delivery time, shipping time, and packaging. If something doesn't meet your expectations, you can always change it quickly. You will probably have to go through a couple of samples until you find one that fits your needs.

Step 9: Product Pricing

Now that you have everything ready, the next step is to price your t-shirts. Not just that, you need to write product descriptions as well. How do you price your products? The price will depend on the cost that the fulfillment company will charge you. A print fulfillment company makes a profit on the base fee that they charge per product. Look at this example for the price of a t-shirt: $10 (t-shirt) + $5 (shipping)= $15. You can add up your markup cost to the base price of the fulfillment company. If you want to make a profit of $10, you can sell the t-shirts at $20 and add another $5 for shipping. The base price of the t-shirts will depend on the brand and the quality of the material. So, you need to try out a couple of pricing policies before you find one that meets your requirements. Once you have a price in mind, you must write the product descriptions. Try to make the descriptions seem as interesting as possible. For instance, you can write about your inspiration for the idea, or even something quirky about the t-shirt. Or you can advise on how you can style the t-shirt. Provide information about the material and sizing. Sizing is an essential aspect, and you must be careful about it. Mention the cut and fit of the t-shirt as well. Since the customer cannot see the physical product in real time, you must make your description as detailed as possible.

Well, now all you need to do is get your store up and running!

Chapter Twelve: Social Media Marketing

Best Platforms

There are few people who have not heard of the likes of Facebook and Twitter but there are other social media platforms that, used in the right way, can be very effective in your marketing campaign. We are going to look at the top social media platforms and how they can help your social media marketing campaign.

Facebook

Facebook is undeniably the most popular social media platform there is these days and it has over 1.2 billion active users. It is a great advertising platform for all businesses since it offers both free and paid advertising options. It also offers you the opportunity to create a business profile, and you must use it to keep in touch with your target audience. You can also use this platform to build your list of subscribers and engage with your audience directly. The advertising system on Facebook is PPC (Pay per click) and it allows you to direct specific ads at your target audience.

Twitter

It is a microblogging and networking platform that has over 200 million active users. It is quite popular amongst celebrities, entrepreneurs, and other businesses to provide regular updates. The regular updates are known as Tweets and a tweet cannot exceed 140 characters. This restriction on text certainly makes it quite compatible with the SMS system. You can create a Twitter profile for your business and use it to attract followers.

Instagram

Instagram is an extremely popular social media site these days and is meant for sharing visual media. You can share photo as well as video media on this platform. Instagram boasts over 150 million active monthly users. It is a great platform for all businesses that like to engage with their audience through visual media. A business can post photos and videos of their products, behind-the-scenes glimpses, and even use it as a promotional tool.

YouTube

YouTube has grown into an influential social media platform. What started out as a fun medium of introducing the world to three-dimensional interaction has now turned into a powerful tool of marketing. Just like every other social media channel, the secret to success is getting a following or audience to broadcast your videos to. The more views you get, the more popular your videos will be and the greater success you will have in ranking highly in search results.

People can comment on your videos and even share them across other platforms like Twitter, Google+, or Facebook.

Tips

If you have decided that social media marketing is the way to go for your business, you will find these tips invaluable.

Select the right platform

If you want to use social media to promote your business, then you need to select the perfect platform for this purpose. You need to opt for a platform that a majority of your target audience uses actively. It doesn't make sense to promote your business on a platform that your target audience hardly uses. Also, it isn't a good idea to use all the platforms of social media to promote your business. Not only is it difficult to do so, but it can be quite expensive in terms of time and funds spent.

Always evaluate

There is a lot of data available these days about performance metrics, your audience, and your business. You need to evaluate all the data. There are some social media platforms that provide analytical tools that you can use for this purpose. Apart from this, there are several third-party apps and services that you can use to analyze the data you collect. You can use metrics like views, shares, and comments on your social media profile to design your marketing campaign. Social media marketing is about increasing the reach of your business.

Timing

The content that you post is critical, but that's not what social marketing is all about. You need to work to increase the interaction your audience has with your posts. So, it is important that you time your posts. You need to post at a time when you know that a majority of your audience will be active on your chosen platform.

Establish Connections

A common mistake that a lot of social media marketers make is that they don't interact with their audience. You need to interact with your audience and engage them. You cannot build a loyal customer base for your business if you don't talk to your audience. The audience needs to know that they are communicating with a human being and not an automated bot. Don't engage in a monologue, instead strive to strike a dialogue with your audience.

Visual route

Large blocks of text can be rather off-putting. So, instead go the visual route and use lots of images, videos, and infographics in your marketing campaign. All these visual means are not only appealing but are easy to understand as well. Even if you write a brilliant essay, no one has the time or patience to go through it.

Make the Platforms Unique

A person who is following your business on one platform might follow you on some other platform as well. So, while you repurpose your content, make sure that you aren't merely posting the same content everywhere. For instance, the content that you use on FB can be repurposed for your campaign on YouTube or Snapchat. You can use similar content, but don't make it repetitive. Not just that, you need to customize the content according to the platform that you choose to use. The images that you use on Snapchat cannot be repurposed for Instagram.

Be appreciative

You need to understand that everyone likes to be acknowledged. In fact, it is a basic human desire to feel appreciated. So, you can offer rewards to your followers for subscribing or following you. It can be something as simple as a thank you or even a special discount. People need to know that their support is appreciated. You need to make it worthwhile for your audience to follow you.

Be personable

Social media is certainly a more relaxed manner of marketing than conventional marketing methods. It doesn't mean that you completely forego all sorts of professionalism. You need to be personable on social media for others to like you. Try to engage in some harmless and engaging banter with your audience. You can ask them for their opinions on certain topics and provide them some personal information that will lend a human touch to your business.

Social Media Manager

If you think you cannot handle a social media marketing campaign, then you can always hire a social media manager who will do the work for you. It is always a good idea to reach out for additional help when you know that you cannot do something by yourself.

Walk away

If you feel that a certain aspect of the social media marketing strategy is not working for your business, then ditch it. It is quite likely that everything will not work out favorably for you.

If something doesn't work, cut your losses and ditch it. Instead, you can focus all your resources on a campaign that seems to be working well for you.

Network

Use social media to not just network with your audience, but other businesses in your niche or industry. It is always a good idea to build relations with other businesses (not your direct competitors).

It is not just a slice of the marketing pie

Most marketers tend to believe that social media is nothing but another platform that businesses and brands can use to distribute their message. Yes, social media does help you with this, but that's not the sole purpose it serves. If you keep using your social media to only post promotional content, then you will certainly end up as social media road kill. You need to use your social media accounts to familiarize the account with your brand and use it to increase your reach. For instance, if your business has a profile on Instagram and all that you do on it is give sales pitches, you will quickly lose followers and it will not do you any good.

Social-Media Experts

It is always a good idea to hire a social media expert whenever you need some additional help. One thing that you need to be wary of are the so-called social media experts who are all talk. A lot of these people can certainly talk the talk but cannot walk the walk. If someone claims to be an expert or an authority on social media, then they need to support such claims with sufficient evidence and quantifiable results. If you think that you can manage your social media campaigns by yourself, then please go ahead and do so.

Somethings Never Change

In the recent past, the world of marketing has undergone tremendous change. It doesn't mean that the old-fashioned rules about communication, PR and marketing don't hold true anymore. These basic ethics can never go out of fashion. It is imperative to understand your target audience; the value you can add to their lives and the purpose your business serves. You need to consider all this if you want to develop an effective marketing strategy. Also, you must never forget that social media is only a small part of your marketing strategy and not the entire strategy. So, don't stray away from these values when you consider the option of social media marketing. If you want your social media marketing campaign to be successful, then there are various elements that need to come together perfectly. All the elements of your campaign need to be in a symbiotic relation with each other. Social media is just one element of your campaign and you need to make all other elements work together seamlessly. You must use the traditional methods of marketing and try to incorporate social media marketing into them.

Chapter Thirteen: Affiliate Marketing

It can be quite difficult to sell a product or market a service, especially when you cannot reach your target audience. At times, you need different means to sell your products, or you might need to make some extra money. In such cases, you must opt for affiliate marketing. In affiliate marketing, a vendor sells their products or services with the help of an affiliate. The affiliate will help to market and promote the products to potential customers. It will help the vendor make a sale, and the vendor will pay the affiliate a certain fee for the effort they make. Affiliate marketing is quite prevalent these days. It can be something as simple as writing a review for a product or service on a social media platform. In this section, you will learn about selecting an affiliate program and earning money from affiliate marketing.

Selecting an Affiliate Program

Avoid Paid-for Programs

A simple Google search for "affiliate marketing programs" will provide you tens of thousands of hits. Some companies will ask you to pay a fee to join their program. All the fancy downloadable applications include well-thought-out payment plans. Not just that, they even try to hype their fee by giving you a so-called "discount" on their fee or other "special plans" to lure unsuspecting users. If you ever come across such a website, you must run in the opposite direction. When you search for affiliate programs, trust your gut. An affiliate program will not provide you a commission unless you make a sale. Remember that they need your help to make the deal. So, why must you pay the company to provide them with your advice? It doesn't make any sense, does it? Steer clear such websites that ask you to pay a fee to join their affiliate program. Don't ever give out your credit card details and you certainly must not make an online banking transaction on a website that seems spurious.

Check the Business

Any affiliate program you wish to join must add value to your site. It must be something that visitors to your site will find useful. If you want to increase website traffic, then you must look for those affiliates that go well with your website. You have complete autonomy to select the affiliate you want to work with. You can check a couple of sites or blogs to see the kind of affiliates they host. Once you know what you are looking for, you can contact them yourself. Make a list of businesses that you would like to associate yourself with. Once you do this, the next thing you must do is check if the website is user-friendly. Try to think about the affiliate program from the perspective of your audience. Will they want to click on the link? If so, then how easy is it to complete a transaction? You must believe in the website before you decide to endorse it to your users. You can place an order on the site and see the process for yourself. You can lose your audience if you provide them with links that seem out of place or unnecessary to them.

The Terms and Conditions

If you are happy and confident about the company or business you select, you must go through their terms and conditions.

You must be aware of all their terms and conditions before you decide to get involved with them. Understand how the program works, the commission you will receive, as well as the terms of the contract. Understand the payment mechanism. You can even set a commission rate for yourself. Money is an essential aspect of affiliate marketing. After all, you are using your audience base to improve the sales of the company. You deserve a good commission for the effort you make. Carefully read through the clauses regarding rights and obligations, along with termination clauses. Accept it only when you feel that it is worth your while.

Earn from Affiliate Marketing

If you want to build a passive stream of income for yourself from affiliate marketing, it will take considerable time and effort. Don't expect to be successful overnight. Here are a couple of things that will help you to increase your earnings from affiliate marketing.

Build Your Website Traffic

Affiliate marketing thrives on people's interest in clicking on links to products that catch their eye. But who are these "people"? Well, these are people who will visit your blog or website to read what you have written. So in order to lure these people, you have to make your blog or site as interesting as possible. It is fine to go all out and decorate it as much as you like. But make sure you keep with the theme otherwise people will only visit to mock your blog. You need to have a good readership or audience base if you want to venture into affiliate marketing. If you don't have a readership, who will you be marketing to? Not just that, why will a company or a business even want to make use of your services if you don't have a good reach? Spend some time building your PR. It will help in increasing your reach and the greater the number of people who are aware of you and your services, the higher your chances of being successful in affiliate marketing. So, you obviously must not create your own website tonight and join an affiliate marketing program tomorrow. It doesn't make any sense.

A good product or service will do

Newcomers to the system often make the mistake of peppering their site or sites with lots of different things, imagining that people are likely to buy more because they have more choice. You are not a store – you don't have to offer your customers choice, because they did not land on your site with purchase in mind. Think of yourself as a pop up store to promote one product as opposed to a super market that offers a lot of choices.

It is always the power of suggestion that works on a majority of customers. They will take a liking to something if you tell them that you are offering them the same product that you have personally tested and liked yourself. If you have put up just one product or service and the website is offering it at the best price in the market then even if the person has left your site to do a quick price comparison, he or she is sure to return back to yours to click on the ad. Also, focusing on a single product or business makes it easier to make keywords work for you.

Content is crucial

Viewers go to websites to be informed or entertained – often both at the same time. So, make sure you have plenty of content structured around the products or business you are promoting. Another point to remember is that search engines can tell whether there's quality content on your site, and will rank it higher as a result. That means more visitors, and hopefully more sales. You need to work on SEO as well. It refers to search engine optimization. You can improve your online visibility by increasing your SEO as well. You must select all the top words or keywords from your blog or website, that are most likely going to be typed by people. But remember just a good SEO description will not do the trick and you need to have good content as well.

The content you are offering must not just be interesting; it needs to be engaging as well. Also, make sure that the content consists of different topics and not just one genre. You can attract and improve your audience base by doing this. You must also make sure that the quality of the content you are offering stays the same throughout. Viewers will stop visiting your website or blog if your content isn't of good quality. Don't bombard your users with too many links and promos. The subtle power of suggestion works better than flooding them with affiliate links.

Promote your Site

Without proper promotion, how are you going to get word about your website out there? There are only so many friends that will click on your links in order for you to land a major gig. Start by listing your site on search engines, write press releases to be distributed online, and promote your site on forums in your niche and social media. If you have a friend whose blog is extremely popular then you can ask him or her to subtly promote yours on theirs. Ideally, choose another blog that speaks on topics like yours or something along the same lines. Make use of various social media platforms for increasing your website's popularity as well. Work on building an army of followers, but don't ever consider buying them. Followers who are bought aren't going to go to your website and click on the affiliate links – they simply provide the false illusion that your social media account is more popular than it is. You might think that you are popular, but once that bubble bursts, you might be extremely disappointed. So, try to find a diverse group who will not lose interest in your writing and don't force anyone or buy anyone for the job. You cannot cheat your readers or your marketing partners. Remember, you will reap what you sow, and so it is best that you remain as honest and trustworthy as possible.

Don't be invisible or anonymous

A golden rule of online marketing is that you must not be invisible or anonymous. You must have confidence in who you are and what you do. If you don't have the necessary self-confidence, then don't expect things will work in your favor. Think of a scenario where you have to address an important crowd consisting of your potential clients and you don't have the confidence to reveal your true identity. Well, that certainly must not work out well for you. It might be quite easy to hide behind an alias on the web, but that doesn't mean you must do this. If you want to build your online credibility, then you must not hide behind a really cool username. Instead, you must focus on making your true persona known to as many people as you possibly can. If you want to use a pen name, then make sure that your real name is included in brackets beside the pen name. Make sure you write out your full name including initials, as there can be many others with the same name as you.

People need to know they can contact you with questions, and that they will get an answer from a real person. They might also ask for a genuine photograph just to be sure of who the other person is. If they aren't confident about your blog or website, then it is highly unlikely that they will even want to click on any affiliate links that you advertised on your blog. Make sure that you reply to any queries that a user posts. You can't trust a client who must not reply to your queries, will you? Well, the same applies to other users as well. People will be wary of doubting a person who doesn't even reveal his or her true identity.

Affiliate is a wonderful way in which you can monetize your website, blog, or any other online portal, and earn money online. It helps you to create a perpetual stream of passive income. However, it is not just about signing up and getting started. You need to check what is on offer and be certain that you are happy and comfortable with the particular service or product that you are promoting. Remember, you need to put in considerable time and effort if you want to earn good returns.

Don't start flooding your web space with lots of affiliate links for various products. It is likely that your readers will be put off because they will feel like they are being spammed. So, try to restrict the number of links you provide your readers. Make use of a soft sell approach, create good content for engaging your readers, and then you can gradually steer them towards affiliate links. When done properly, affiliate marketing can be quite enjoyable and lucrative. However, it does take some time for building up your online presence as well as trust, so don't think about rushing things. Take time for getting everything right, and soon you can start enjoying a steady stream of passive income through affiliate marketing.

Chapter Fourteen: Impulse Buying

Impulsive buyers are buyers who make a purchase on a whim and without any planning. A purchase that is made on the spur of the moment that provides instant gratification to the buyer is an impulse purchase. Impulsive buyers can be a boon for any business. As a drop shippers, you will need to work hard to encourage impulsive buying. In this section, you will learn about a couple of ways in which you can promote impulsive buying.

Conditional Free Shipping

Free shipping can be quite compelling and can help increase the value for an online shopper. You can use this to your advantage while you structure your shipping offer. Calculate the average order value and make it around $20-$50 and you can offer free shipping if a purchase is between these amounts. Take a moment and think about it. If you want to buy something online and your purchase amounts to $40, but the shipping charges are $5, then you will hesitate for a moment about the purchase. Instead, you can offer conditional free shipping if the shopper makes a purchase for a specific amount like $40. You can even encourage shoppers by coming up with a couple of suggestions in the specific price group during checkout to encourage them to meet the conditional limit.

Sales and Promotions

Incentives as well as special pricing will help increase impulse purchases. You can use a sale or promotion to encourage customers to make a purchase just like you use free shipping. Often, in a physical retail outlet, low-priced items are the ones that are often purchased. Similarly, you can come up with a sale to drive impulse purchases.

Mobile Optimization

A main reason that encourages customers to impulsively buy something is that online shopping is quick and easy. So, if someone decides to make an unplanned purchase, then a slow and tedious buying process will be off putting. You need to ensure that your website is streamlined and is optimized for mobile usage. You can even develop a mobile app to help you with this.

Web Design

There is a direct relationship that exists between impulse buying and the quality of the website. You need to make sure that your website design is of high-quality. The website needs to look appealing to a buyer and it is quite likely that the customer will end up buying something.

Chapter Fifteen: Product Listings

Product listing refers to the listing of all the products in a particular category and is also known as category pages. Usually, customers tend to review product listings before selecting a specific product.

In this section, you will learn about product listings on your website.

Information

A common question that a lot of business owners have while listing their products is what information must be displayed for individual products on the listing page and what must be displayed on the product page? The two important things that you must consider while determining the answer to this question are:

The category page must always include all the possible information that a customer will need to choose between the available products. According to the customer segment, this information will vary. So, you need to have all the necessary information regarding the style, budget, or any other unique feature of the product to help the customer make a decision. The information that you provide on the category pages for the products needs to be precise and you must avoid unnecessary information. Try to limit the content on this page since your main idea is to fit as many products on a page as you possibly can. It helps make the list more usable for the customer. In fact, it is better to not include any information that isn't necessary for selection; instead you can use the information on the product page.

Photos, Icons and Graphics

To make your category page appealing, you need to include high-quality photos of products. A picture is certainly worth a thousand words, so choose pictures wisely to avoid the need for extra product information. While including the product information, try not to overwhelm the viewer. The photos you use must be sized properly so that you can display a lot of products on each page. Also, the images you use must not be flashy and must not be airbrushed. You will need to deal with a lot of unhappy customers if you use images that make the product appear better than they are.

You can even use icons for your store, provided that they are all structured around a single type of product, meaning much of the product information you include is similar for all products. If that's the case, then you can create a system of icons that you can use.

Number of Products per Row

The number of products that you want to list in a row will depend on the information that need to be displayed about a product. It essentially depends on the different qualities that a customer might want to use to select something along with whether the customer finds those qualities desirable or not. The usual practice is to list one product in a row and is often wasteful. So, list only one product per row if you think the information you are providing is absolutely necessary. There are stores that list five or even six products in a row, but this is not desirable. When you list so many products in a row, the product image tends to become too small and the scope to display information is drastically reduced. You need to strike a balance between these two extremes. Ideally, it is good practice to display about two or three images in a row.

Number of Products per Page

The number of products that you list on a category page is the next aspect of product listing you need to decide. It is convenient to scroll through a page instead of waiting for the next page to load. So, you can include as many products as you want on a page. Usually, websites display around ten products per page, even if they list only one product per row. Until a couple of years ago, businesses used to avoid displaying a lot of products on a page because of the long download time. A lot of products meant a lot of pictures and it meant the page used to take a while to download. Well, now all this is a concern of the past. With the introduction of high-speed Internet connections, it hardly takes a fraction of a second to display a webpage. Ideally, try to stick to less than 50 products per page.

A lot of category pages have a dropdown list that allows the customer to select the number of products that they will want to view at any given time. The Items per Page dropdown menu must list the multiples of the number of products that are displayed in a row. For instance, if you decide to display 5 images in a row, then the Items per Page numbers must include 10, 20, 30, 40, and so on.

Sorting

You must always provide your customers with the option of sorting the product display on the page. When you do this, it makes the category pages quite effective and easy to navigate.

Not just that, it also helps the customers view the products that meet their specific criteria. Sorting options must always be based on the information or the features that will be relevant to your target audience.

When the customer has the option to sort the products according to a specific quality they are looking for, it is easier to narrow down the number of appropriate items and also requires less filtering. It is a good idea to provide different sorting options to your customers apart from the default sort order. There are two reasons why the default sort order is important. The first reason is that, even though a customer can change this order, most customers tend to use this default setting. The second reason is that you can control the default sort order and it is similar to a list of recommendations.

Chapter Sixteen: Scaling

In this section, you will learn about the ways in which you can scale your dropshipping business.

A lot of people simply assume that you need to use only Facebook ads for scaling up your business. In fact, there are different ways in which you can do this. Your odds of succeeding at scaling your business are directly proportional to the number of scaling strategies that you have in your marketing arsenal. You can scale your business in the following ways:

Sales teams include cold calling and cold emailing procedures. You can use Facebook lookalike audiences, similar audiences on Google, using different types of advertising platforms, you can recruit a team of affiliate marketers to promote your business, work with top influencers on social media, you can also increase your budget for advertising in small installments, duplicate winning ad campaigns to target the same or new audience, and franchising or creating duplicates of your store in different places.

The one thing that is common for all these methods is that they will enable you to obtain new customers and increase your sales in a predictable manner. There is no upper limit to the number of customers you can obtain from these methods and they will certainly increase your sales too. So, how else can you scale your business?

You can scale your business horizontally, which means that you will be going wider instead of deeper. For instance, let us assume that you spend about $5 per day for a Facebook ad and that specific ad set is doing well. One way in which you can scale the ad set is to increase your daily budget in small installments. So, instead of finding new audience you will just increase your ad budget to an ad set that is doing well. This is an example of scaling vertically. Alternatively, you can duplicate this ad set, or you can create multiple ads that are similar and try to target new pages on Facebook that you haven't explored yet. When you do this, you are scaling wider instead of vertically.

The best way to scale up your dropshipping business horizontally is to use the franchising technique. It is a good method to scale your dropshipping business. No, it isn't about KFC or Starbucks outlets, but you can use a similar method to scale your existing dropshipping business. Instead of trying to expand your customer base in one country, you will need to duplicate the entire store in a new country and target a newer audience.

For instance, if you have a dropshipping store in USA, you can use Facebook ads to target your ideal customers. Once this store starts to do well, you decide to duplicate this store in another country, like Spain, you need someone to translate your English store and all the ads into Spanish. You will also need to hire someone to take care of customer support. Once you do this, your store will start to do well in Spain as well. This is an example of scaling your business horizontally. You can expand your business to as many countries as you want to and possibly can. Make sure that you have someone around who can communicate fluently in the local language of the country you decide to set up a store in for customer support. If not, you can always hire help for this purpose.

You might or might not want to scale up your business with multiple stores. So, what can you do in such a situation? Can you keep your dropshipping store and use it to target a worldwide audience? You most certainly can do this. In fact, this is the second method in which you can scale up your business.

It is less efficient than duplicating the store and translating all ads and content. The greater number of stores you have, the Facebook ads and the marketing tools you use are tailored for the specific audience you are targeting. In such a case, the rate of conversion is also higher. For instance, if you have a store in Germany or Spain, then people have the option of shopping in their native language and the currency they use. The storefront is tailor-made to suit their needs and requirements. It doesn't mean that you will not have any customers if your global store is in English and the currency you use is USD. If someone doesn't like to pay in USD, is suspicious of purchasing something from a foreign store or doesn't speak English, then such a customer will not make a purchase.

So, which of these strategies can you use to scale your store? The answer to this question depends on the number of countries you plan to target. If your store is successful in one language and you are fluent in another language as well, then it is a good idea to duplicate the store. The one thing that you need to keep in mind is that duplication of a store takes a lot of work and, therefore, the number of countries you can target is quite low. You can also get higher rates of conversion, but the potential of scalability reduces.

On the other hand, if you have one global store, then you can duplicate your best-performing ad sets and target various other countries, but the conversion rate will be lower. But, it does offer you the opportunity to scale wider.

The best way to decide which of these methods will work for your business is to try them! Start with a global store and then see how things work for you.

Chapter Seventeen: Passive Income and Virtual Assistants

If you want a source of passive income, then it is important that you outsource certain daily tasks. In this section, you will learn about how, when, and why you must outsource. Apart from this, you will also learn to hire, train, and manage remote virtual assistants.

Why do you need a virtual assistant?

The first reason why you need a virtual assistant (VA) is because time is an invaluable asset and in business time is money. For instance, if you have to take care of several businesses or have to juggle between a regular job and dropshipping, then a VA will make your life easier. If you spend all your time handing complaints, responding to emails, dealing with service requests, or even fulfilling orders, you will not have time left to manage and grow your businesses. A virtual assistant will take care of all the repetitive tasks that don't require your presence. It will help you optimally utilize your valuable time.

When to hire a VA?

Don't hire a virtual assistant in the beginning. You will need a VA once your business starts to process over 10-15 orders per day. In the beginning, you can take care of all the aspects of your dropshipping business like market research, customer support and everything else involved. In fact, it is a good idea that you do all this by yourself initially. It will give you an idea of how things work and what you need to do. In fact, you must do all of this occasionally even after you hire a VA.

What Positions are VA's Suitable for?

The first VA you decide to hire needs to handle a couple of aspects of the dropshipping business like handling business communication (responding to emails, comments and messages), customer support and order fulfillment. You need to find a VA who has a good knowledge of the dropshipping business. Once your store starts to grow and the orders, support requests, and business communication increase, you can hire other virtual assistants according to the work. The second VA you hire can take care of all aspects of business communication and can eventually start doing all the market research and add new products to the product list. In this manner, you can edit the description of all the new products and launch your ads. All this saves time. You don't need to hire any full-time virtual assistants and you need them for about 1-3 hours per day.

Delegation might not be something that comes to you naturally. If you want to automate your business and convert your dropshipping enterprise into a passive stream of income, then you need virtual assistants. In this section, you will learn about the different ways in which you can hire a virtual assistant and the tasks that you can delegate.

Tasks you Can Outsource

The dropshipping business is quite lucrative and it provides you an opportunity to be your own boss. There are various perks of dropshipping business and you can work on it while holding onto a regular 9-5 job. Initially, everything might seem quite peachy and exciting, but what will happen when you try to expand your business? The workload will increase and the number of things you need to handle will increase as well. All this can be quite overwhelming. What is the solution to this problem? The solution is quite simple, and it is outsourcing. Outsourcing is the process of making someone outside your business handle certain aspects of your business instead of doing it in-house. The good news is that there are several aspects of the dropshipping business that you can outsource to free up your time and reduce your workload.

You can pretty much outsource all the aspects of your business, but here are the top tasks that you can easily outsource.

Market Research

The first task that you can outsource is market research. It takes a lot of time and effort to research the items that will prove to be profitable for your business. Market research is an ongoing process and you cannot stop doing this once you start your business. You must not only look for newer products, but you must check your competition and evaluate the different platforms that you can use for your business.

Product Listing

Another task that can take up a lot of time is product listing on your store. You can outsource this responsibility and, in fact, you can hire a professional to do this work for you.

Data Entry

Let us face it, data entry is a simple task, but it is quite time consuming and cumbersome. Data entry is an important part of your research and you can outsource it these days.

Customer Service

Ideally, it is a good idea to handle customer service by yourself. As a business owner, it makes more sense to outsource this task to someone else. Instead of spending all your time answering queries, responding to mails, dealing with returns, and providing assistance to customers, you can concentrate on something else.

Content

Good content is critical for your business. You need content for not just your website, but for product descriptions, social media posts, and even any other blog posts you want to make. It can take up a lot of your precious time. You can instead hire a copywriter to help you create exceptional content.

Optimize Product Titles

Another task that you can take off your plate is optimizing product listings. You can hire a freelancer to do this work for you.

There are other tasks that you can outsource like building and maintaining your website, emailing potential clients and suppliers, managing your schedule, HTML templates for product listings, and graphics for your images and logos too.

So, where can you find reliable workers for all this? The three best websites that you can hire trustworthy freelancers from are Upwork, Freelancer, and Fiverr.

Hire a Virtual Assistant

Post a Job

The best way to find a VA is through your network and ask for referrals. It is always better to look for people who come with a recommendation. You can look for VA's by posting an ad for the same on different platforms like Slack, LinkedIn or even Facebook. Social media is the best way to reach anyone. Apart from this, there are different platforms that you can use to find a virtual assistant like Upwork, Zirtual, and UAssistMe. You can also use freelance marketplaces like Guru, TaskPigeon, PeoplePerHour, and Freelancer to find a VA for your dropshipping business.

Whenever you post an ad, you need to make sure that it is precise, engaging, and includes the key phrases that a potential VA might look for like customer service assistant or business communications assistant. To save time in the weeding out process and qualifying applicants, you can as, the applicants, give the answer to a random question in the first line of reply. If you do this, it will help to review only those applicants you took the time that read the job post thoroughly. The job description you give in the post is quite important when you are trying to attract the right candidates. You need to include a couple of details like business volume, the apps and the platforms your business uses, any language requirements, and the specific tasks they will need to perform.

Shortlist and Interview

Once you go through all the applications you receive, the next step is to shortlist the candidates and schedule interviews. You can use any of the video platforms like Skype or Google

Hangouts to conduct the interview. The interview must not last for longer than 30 minutes and you need to prepare a questionnaire. You need to include certain vital questions to determine the skillset and the mindset of the applicant. You must remember that you can always teach a person a new skill, but you cannot change their mindset.

The questions you can ask the applicant are:

What do they enjoy doing? What are the skills that you want them to learn or perfect? What are their strengths? What made them respond to your ad? What do they usually do in their free time? What is their educational background?

Once you are certain that you have chosen the perfect candidate, the next step is to discuss payment. Usually, virtual assistants get paid anywhere between $5 per hour to $25 per hour. If you decide to hire someone from Upwork you can set up an hourly contract with them and the payment will be directly wired to them according to the number of hours they clock.

It is a good idea to give your VA a trial task to observe their skills. If the VA passes the test, you can offer a trial period for two weeks to test the VA's capabilities. If things go well, then you can start delegating manual tasks to the VA.

On-boarding

Usually, candidates tend to exit during the trail period. So, it is a good idea to get the two VA's onboard simultaneously. You will have the opportunity to witness whether they are as good as they claim to be or not. The best-case scenario is that you might end up with two good VA's in the end.

Guidelines

You need to create a training manual as well as written guidelines for the on-boarding process. You can use certain videos or recording to go together with the written guides to train your VA. If you are training a VA, make sure that you record the training sessions and you can use them to train future VA's.

Training

There are different online resources that you can use to train remote virtual assistants to do specific tasks or use specific tools. For instance, HubSpot Academy is one of the best online places to learn about things like content creation, web designing, email marketing, and the like. HubSpot offers several engaging and detailed online classes to learn about the different aspects of running an online business. Another resource that you can use to teach your VAs about SEO is Moz's Beginner's Guide to SEO. SEO increases the online visibility of your business and is an important area that you need to concentrate on. Use the above-mentioned tool to teach your VAs about how they can research for keywords, learn the way search engines work, and also learn to measure and track the success rate of their keywords.

If you use any form of paid advertising and you want to teach your VA to manage it, then you can use WordStream's PPC University to get them better acquainted with paid advertising campaigns. This is a great place for anyone who wants to learn about CTR, CPC, negative keywords, split-advertisement testing, and all other aspects of PPC advertising. A couple of other platforms you can use to train your Virtual Assistants are Social Media Quickstarter, CodeAcademy, and Canva's Design School.

Management

Your job doesn't end once you hire a VA. You not only need to ensure that the work goes smoothly, but you also need to make sure that you nurture this relationship. It is your responsibility to make sure the VA is satisfied with his or her job profile and is learning things that will benefit the VA as well as your business. If your VA starts to lose interest or the relationship becomes stale, then it is likely that the VA will quit, To ensure that this doesn't happen, you need to effectively manage the virtual assistants. You can ask the VA to send you a weekly update about all the things that they have achieved and the tasks they have completed. You can also schedule weekly calls and go over the projects or tasks you want the VA to perform and discuss those areas in which they excelled and the ones you want them to improve on. The greater the trust that you establish, the lesser time is necessary to supervise and motivate your VA to work.

Ideally, you need to develop a working relationship where the VA works independently. Doing this will not only help in the growth of the VA, but it will also make you comfortable with delegating complex responsibilities.

Communication

There are different apps and platforms that you can use to communicate with your VA. Here are a couple of apps and platforms that you can use for this purpose.

If you want to create projects and then assign them to a group of VAs or a team, then you can use Asana. Slack is an amazing platform for not just communication but even collaboration for all work-related tasks. If you want to create to-do lists, then

Trello is the app for you. Use YouCanBook.Me for scheduling meetings in a simple and quick manner. If you want to text and chat for free while on the go, then WhatsApp must be your go-to app. Use Skype or Google Hangouts for making video calls. If you want to share files or any other documents, then Google Drive is the best option available these days.

Delegation

Delegation isn't something that comes easy for a lot of people. In fact, it can be quite difficult for a business owner to start delegating tasks. It can be difficult to entrust your business responsibilities to someone else, especially when you have built everything up from the scratch. If you want to expand or build a team for yourself, then delegation is quite important. You can free up your valuable time to concentrate on the important aspects of business with the help of a VA. You need to create a work system that not only works for you but works for your VA as well. The goal is to free up your time so that you can concentrate on the things that matter. It might take you a while until you find someone who you trust and get along well with. Hiring a VA will certainly be worth all the hassle that you go through.

Investment

You need to understand that your VA is an investment and you must treat the VA accordingly. VA is an investment of your time as well as money. You need to consider that your business might last longer than you. If you want to build a personal brand, then you need a VA to help you along the way. Take a moment to think about some strong personal brands present in business. Names like Steve Jobs and Richard Branson come up quite often. Even though Steve Jobs is long gone, his reputation lives on and will live for a long time. It isn't just Jobs, but even Branson's reputation will outlive him as well. These leaders have a persona that ooze originality, creativity, and something else that makes them quite special.

If you hire a VA, then you will have some assistance while building your personal brand. In fact, think of hiring a VA as an investment on behalf of your business. You need to spend time to train and develop the VA so that they can generate ROI.

Chapter Eighteen: Advertising and Dropshipping

Build Trust

The first thing you can do to advertise your dropshipping business is build trust by adding customer reviews and testimonials to your website. First-time shoppers usually are skeptical about the quality of the products listed on the website. If you add some promising customer reviews, testimonials and ratings to your business website, then it will build the visitor's trust. For instance, the drop shippers on Aliexpress usually include a snapshot of the customer's feedback to their website. You can also use the reviews present on your supplier's store and add it to your website. If you want to expand your business, then it is a good idea to build your own set of testimonials, reviews, and ratings.

Facebook ads

There are more than two million active users on Facebook every month. You need to leverage the reach of this platform to advertise your dropshipping business. Facebook is a favorite platform for a lot of dropshipping businesses because of the diversity and the rich data it collects. It means that you can be as specific as you want while targeting ads on Facebook. Facebook ads offer a high degree of customizability. So, you can ensure that the right ads reach the desired audience. You can customize these ads according to your budget, goal and audience. You can also choose the format of the ads and select the places where you want to display the ad. The ads you run on Facebook can also be run on Messenger, Instagram, and Audience Network. If you want your Facebook ads campaign to be successful, then you need to invest in good video content. Video content is a great means to reach your potential audience and encourage them to interact with your brand. Video content is easier to understand and remember than textual content. Use Facebook ads to target all those on your contact list and your email list.

Share Social Videos

Social videos make up for a significant part of the customer web traffic today. A dropshipping business can use video content to promote their business and their products. For instance, MakeBeauty usually shares sneak peeks of how-to videos on their social media accounts and later redirects the viewers to visit their webpage for complete instructional videos. It can be slightly challenging to create social videos, but it will be certainly worth your while. If you don't want to create new videos, then you can search for viral videos on popular sites and use them (don't forget to give due credit and seek permissions). You can then use call-to-action buttons on these videos to direct traffic to your dropshipping website.

Retargeting

Most visitors don't usually make a purchase on their first visit. This can be a major hurdle for dropshipping websites since gaining traffic is not easy. In such a situation, you can use retargeting to recapture the visitor's attention. Retargeting is a simple marketing technique that targets previous visitors to your website who didn't take any action. It is your chance to capture an apparently lost opportunity. Once you retarget such visitors, it is quite likely that your sales will increase.

Blog

You can start a blog to drive organic traffic to your business website. Blogs are frequently looked up to as sources of information. Blog marketing is a low-cost marketing strategy that will help you reach your target audience. The primary benefit of blog marketing for your business is that it helps you build your audience while generating more organic traffic to your business website. Another vital benefit of blog marketing is that it helps SEO results. SEO refers to Search Engine Optimization and is the process of enhancing the online visibility of your business. You can streamline your blog entries for SEO results.

Identify Your Niche

You need to identify where your niche usually hangs around and try to join that group. A niche represents a community with a shared interest. All dropshipping businesses usually have a niche. You need to take advantage of this and make yourself a part of a niche and it offers a platform to connect with others who share a similar interest.

Upsell and Cross-Sell

You can encourage the shoppers to shop more with upselling and cross-selling marketing. A dropshipping business needs to maximize every transaction that's conducted. Usually, these two techniques are used synonymously, but there is a slight difference between the two. Both help increase the chances of impulsive buying and combining them into one strategy is a good idea.

Chapter Nineteen: Get Started

It might seem quite tempting to select five passive income ideas to begin with. However, it is prudent to just stick to one. Every passive income business idea that you can think of requires time and focus for its growth. If you want to create a steady stream of passive income, then you must dedicate the necessary time and attention to your idea. It is better if you master one thing before you move onto another one. Passive income lives up to the hype it has in the market. However, to reach that stage, it takes plenty of time or money. Select an idea, create a plan, and then dedicate yourself to that program, and you certainly can rake in a handsome income. In this section, let us take a look at a couple of tips that you must keep in mind when you get started with a passive income business.

The Reason

Before you start, take a moment and think about the idea that prompted you to opt for the particular stream, or option that you did. Is money the only reason that motivates you? The ability to generate passive income mainly depends on the audience. If the audience detects that it is all about making money for you and not serving their needs, then they won't be too kind to your business idea. Whenever you do something solely for money, you won't succeed. Your intentions need to go beyond acquiring a right bank balance if you want to achieve success. Unless you have a reason that provides you the drive to excel, you will not shine. Money is a byproduct of the desire that keeps you going. So, take some time and think about the reason and motivation for you to do so.

A Lot of Time

The concept of overnight success is mythical, just like unicorns and leprechauns. You cannot expect to become a millionaire overnight. You have to put in all the necessary efforts and dedicate the time required to get there. Do you know that Angry Birds was the 52nd game that Rovio designed? So, even when something might seem like an overnight success, it probably isn't. It takes a while for the business to kick off. However, don't expect results if you don't want to put in the necessary efforts.

Forget About 100% Passive Income

If you think that you can find an income stream that is 100% passive, then you are sadly mistaken. Let go of the thought that once you create a product, you can just bask in the sun and sip margaritas. Even with real estate rentals, you have to manage the property, or with the stock market, you have to continually keep an eye on the portfolio and handle it as well. Even with an online business, there isn't any such thing as 100% passive income. Passive income rests on the concept of the creation of business automation. However, if you want to keep yourself or your business automated, then keep the business going, then you need to put in a lot of time and effort. You cannot earn money without any effort.

Find Your Ideal Market

A lot of business ideas fail because people try to develop a product or build a business that caters to the needs of everyone. When you try to serve everyone around you, you cannot help anyone. You have to select a specialty and then build a niche or search for an existing one. Find a market that suits you or choose a market that you want to cater to. While you select a niche, your target audience takes into consideration your education and your interests as well. Your earnings are proportional to the audience base you serve.

Other Considerations

Before you establish your business idea, you have to think if you will be happy to serve the same market a couple of years from now. Don't select a hot topic just because it seems to perform well at the moment. If you can cater to the same audience but diversify the products you offer, your chances of success will increase as well.

About the Audience

Spend some time to get to know the target audience. Find out about the things that are already available in the market and the gap that your product or service will fill. There might be others who are trying to fill the same service and don't get scared. In fact, the competition that exists kind of validates the need you want to fulfill. There is a market for the product or service you want to offer, so you need to capitalize it as soon as you possibly can. However, that doesn't mean that your work ends there. You have to understand what is unique about the selling proposition you offer and the advantages it has over the other proposals in the market.

Build Your Platform

Now that you know that market you want to cater to, you have to think of a way in which you can share your message. Do you want to do this through a blog, a channel on YouTube, set up a podcast, or is there any other channel that you can think of for the same? You cannot just create a product, service, or business and expect the audience to reach you. You have to build your audience base and then encourage them to utilize the services or products you offer. The entire world doesn't have to follow you. You don't have to serve everyone. If you have 1000 people paying you $100 every year, you can earn $100,000 a year. You don't have to help everyone, just make sure that you can get some value out of those who you serve. Use your platform to build an audience base for yourself. Don't worry even if you cannot reach a lot of people. Concentrate on providing the best you can to those who you can reach. Personalization can come in handy in such cases.

Value

You cannot start to charge your audience immediately. They need to know about the value you offer and not just the value. They need to like what they have to pay for as well. If you want to create a passive income business that is viable in the long run as well, then you must offer value and information for free, at least initially. Let the audience get used to the value you can provide, and once they like it, you can charge them. No one will want to spend their money without being aware of what they can get in return.

Research

Remember always to do a thorough analysis of all the companies that are interested in affiliate marketing. There can be hundreds of them, and you need to do your research on which the best ones are. Even if it takes you forever, you will have to lay down the groundwork for establishing a permanent relationship with a good company. Do not blindly go with the first company that offers you an affiliation. Even if it looks like a good company, wait for other offers to try to weigh out the pros and cons of each company. Rushing into something will only adversely affect you.

Payment

Make sure you talk out everything that there is regarding the amount that you will receive for your services. Some companies will take you for granted and might not pay you enough or on time. You will have to be vigilant and make sure that your account is credited every month. Many people make the mistake of not checking if they are getting money regularly. There might be some companies who will purposely not pay and wait until they are summoned. If they find out that you are not checking, then they will surely take you for a ride. So, make sure you keep track of the money that comes into your account and how many people are reading your blog and how many are clicking on ads. It will mainly be relevant if you are getting paid for leads.

Follow up

Remember to always follow up on all your contracts and agreements. You must have a good rapport with companies and be in constant touch with them. Don't shy away from calling them up or shooting them a mail if you have any doubts or queries. After all, they are tying up with you because they realize your worth. Make sure you follow up on payments and maintain a record of how much money you earn every month.

Interact with those who share your content

Whenever you post some content and if any of your followers share that content, then ensure that you take some time to thank them. These are the people you want on your side- the ones who carry out advertising activities for your business free of cost. Establish and build good relationships with them and make them want to share your content.

Learn the Platform Guidelines

Regardless of the platform you decide to use, you need to familiarize yourself with the guidelines of that platform. You need to learn what is and is not acceptable in terms of behavior as well as content. Take some time and go through the list of terms and conditions of a given platform. Most of the platforms keep updating their terms of service, and make sure that you understand all these terms properly. If you breach any of the terms of service, it can lead to the suspension or removal of your account from that platform.

Include the Location

You must always include your location in your business profile. It can be a physical or a virtual address. If a customer is interested in doing any business with you, then they need to know where they can reach you. Also, include your visiting hours of the business.

Check your Grammar and Spelling

You must always check and then recheck the grammar and spellings of all the content that you decide to post. Proof read the content to weed out any mistakes. Your business's profile on social media is an extension of your business. So, ensure that the content you post is free of any errors.

Please ensure that you keep all the social media marketing tips in mind whenever you design a marketing campaign for your business. By following these simple tips, you can increase your reach and effectiveness of the campaign.

Conclusion

I want to thank you once again for choosing this book.

Dropshipping is a relatively new business model and is quite dynamic. There are different changes that keep taking place in this form of business. So, you need to make sure that you are always updated with the latest trends and business practices. In this book, you were provided with all the basic information that you need to start a dropshipping business. If you have any doubts, then you must refer to the concerned chapter in this book. If you are looking for more in-depth answers to your question, then don't hesitate to search for them on Google or YouTube. You need to soak up as much information as you can about this business model, if you want to be a successful business owner.

Now, all that you need to do is get started. There is no time like the best to start. A wise old man once said, "The best time to plant a tree was ten years ago and the next best time is now."

The idea of starting a new business on your own might seem slightly daunting. All it takes is the first step to obtain the necessary momentum to keep going. So, don't be afraid and take the first step. If you put in the necessary hard work, dedicate sufficient time, and be patient, you will become a successful business owner.

An unfortunate fact is, most businesses fail in their first year, and only a few succeed. If you want to be a part of the successful minority, then you need the necessary motivation, strength, and determination to succeed. Failure must be considered as a stepping-stone to success. If you fail or run into obstacles, just pick yourself up, dust yourself off, and get back in the game. It is not easy, but when you succeed, there is nothing that can replace the high that success gives.

Take everything in your stride and think of it as a learning experience. You can start your passive income journey today, and with the right mindset, it can be easy. The only thing that withholds you is your mindset. Remember that it is never too late to start, and you can always achieve something better for yourself. Don't give up on this feeling and keep it alive throughout your life!

Thank you and all the best!

www.ingramcontent.com/pod-product-compliance
Lightning Source LLC
Chambersburg PA
CBHW050644190326
41458CB00008B/2410